JOHN GAY

The Beggar's Opera
and
Companion Pieces

Crofts Classics

GENERAL EDITORS

On the cover is reproduced an engraving by William Blake, which was published in 1790 after a picture by William Hogarth (1697-1764). The scene is from Act III of *The Beggar's Opera*. Polly, seen singing the song "When my Hero in Court Appears," is the daughter of Peachum, a receiver of stolen goods, who is furious at her marrying the highwayman Macheath, and informs against him. Macheath is brought to Newgate Prison, where he conquers the heart of Lucy, whose father, Lockit, is the warder. From left to right in the engraving are Lucy, Lockit, Macheath, Polly and Peachum. Reproduced by courtesy of the Trustees of the British Museum.

Research for cover art by Nigel Foxell

JOHN GAY

The Beggar's Opera
and
Companion Pieces

EDITED BY

C. F. Burgess

VIRGINIA MILITARY INSTITUTE

AHM PUBLISHING CORPORATION
Northbrook, Illinois 60062

ISBN: 0-88295-037-1

(Formerly 22485-5)

Library of Congress Card Number: 66-16637

CONTENTS

Introduction   vii

Principal Dates in the Life of John Gay   xxi

THE BEGGAR'S OPERA   1

From TRIVIA   74

NEWGATE'S GARLAND   85

'TWAS WHEN THE SEAS WERE ROARING. A BALLAD   88

SWEET WILLIAM'S FAREWELL TO BLACK-EY'D
    SUSAN. A BALLAD   90

MOLLY MOG: OR, THE FAIR MAID OF THE INN   93

AN EPISTLE TO A LADY   96

THE HARE AND MANY FRIENDS   101

From Gay's Letters   103

Bibliography   111

INTRODUCTION

When he had finished reading *The Beggar's Opera* in manuscript sometime during the autumn of 1727, Gay's friend and patron, the Duke of Queensberry, remarked, "This is a very odd thing, Gay. I am satisfied that it is either a very good thing, or a very bad thing." So, too, Alexander Pope and Jonathan Swift, Gay's partners in the triumvirate of Tory Wits, had serious reservations about the play's chances of success. Pope conceded that the play would make "a great noise" but "whether of claps or hisses, I know not." As the time approached for the premiere of *The Beggar's Opera,* he rationalized, in a letter to Swift, "At worst it is in its own nature a thing which he can *lose* no reputation by, as he lays none upon it." Far more disconcerting, however, was the judgment of William Congreve for, if Pope and Swift were uninformed on matters theatrical, the author of *The Way of the World, Love for Love,* and *The Mourning Bride* was recognized and respected as the elder statesman of the stage. Congreve's verdict was that Gay's forthcoming production "would either take greatly, or be damned confoundedly."

Nor was the response of the working professionals, the theatre managers, any more enthusiastic. Gay first submitted the play to Colley Cibber, manager of Drury Lane Theatre, which was then London's most reputable playhouse. Cibber, whose theatrical instincts were usually infallible, was baffled by the "odd thing" that Gay had offered him and somewhat skeptical of its satirical implications which he did not fully fathom. Ultimately, Cibber chose to err on the side of discretion, and he rejected Gay's piece. This action provided one of those intriguing footnotes to English literary history since, for want of a play during the time *The Beggar's Opera* might have been playing at Drury Lane, Cibber turned to *Love in Several Masques,* the maiden effort of a twenty-year-old dramatist, newly arrived in London, Henry Fielding. Nor was John Rich, Cibber's chief rival, to whom Gay next submitted his play, overly sanguine about its prospects. Rich had made a success at the Theatre Royal, the new theatre in Lincoln's Inn Fields, by giving the public low comedy and lavish spectacle, and he was hesitant to abandon this tried and tested formula in favor of Gay's novelty. Only the personal intervention of the influential Duchess of Queensberry on Gay's behalf brought Rich's reluctant consent, and in January, 1728, *The Beggar's Opera* went into rehearsal.

The misgivings of Gay's friends, of Cibber, and of Rich were totally unwarranted. *The Beggar's Opera* was destined to "take greatly"; it was destined, in fact, to make theatrical history. It was to become an authentic classic and the single most popular musical play ever to appear on the English stage.

On January 29, 1728, *The Beggar's Opera* opened at the Theatre Royal in Lincoln's Inn Fields before a glittering audience which by purest chance included one of the main targets of Gay's satire, the Prime Minister of England, Robert Walpole. After an uncertain first act while the theatregoers adjusted to the strangeness of this first English ballad opera, the gusto, vivacity, and charm of Gay's "Newgate pastoral" began to make their appeals, and by the time Macheath's gang sang their marching song, "We Will Take the Road," at the beginning of the second act, it was evident that *The Beggar's Opera* was a resounding success.

To state the case succinctly and without embellishment, *The Beggar's Opera* was a success of proportions never before reached on the London stage. Before the season closed in June, *The Beggar's Opera* had played sixty-two nights, a new first-run record for the English theatre. By today's standards of reckoning theatrical longevity in terms of years, this would seem a modest accomplishment. The true measure of the triumph can be readily gauged, however, by restoring an historical perspective. In Gay's time, single performances for a moderately successful play were not uncommon, and a first run of four to five nights established a play as a definite hit.

The success of *The Beggar's Opera* changed the direction of the English theatre. Until the advent of Gay's comic opus, the Italian Opera, imported from the Continent a generation earlier, was supreme on the London stage. *The Beggar's Opera* and its imitators, literally in the hundreds during the next quarter-century, fixed the popularity of the new genre, the ballad opera. The Italian Opera was left with a relatively limited audience for whom it became something of a social status symbol, a role which foreign-language opera continues to play in English-speaking countries today.

The success of *The Beggar's Opera* also changed the lives of those most immediately responsible for this success. Gay found himself a celebrity overnight, not only as the author of the most popular play of the century but also, because of the play's political overtones, as the champion of the antigovernment cause. "The inoffensive John Gay," Dr. Arbuthnot wrote Swift, "is now become one of the obstructions to the peace of Europe, the terror of the Ministers, the chief author of the *Craftsman* and all the seditious pamphlets which have been published against the government. . . . He is the darling of the city; if he should travel about the country, he would have hecatombs of roasted oxen sacrificed to him." The actors also shared in the play's acclaim. Lavinia Fenton, virtually unknown before her appearance as Polly Peachum, became the toast of the *beau monde* and the special favorite of the galleries. Her portrait was painted by Hogarth; numerous poems (some indifferent, some incredibly bad) were addressed to her; her charms were celebrated in the streets by London's ballad singers; her picture, in engraving, was available everywhere, and, in an eighteenth-century anticipation of modern merchandising methods, "Polly Peachum" fans were all the rage among the ladies. The play's Macheath fared equally well. A nondescript actor before essaying the role of the gallant highwayman, Thomas Walker was transformed into a popular hero by the young bloods of the town. Finally, to his vast delight, *The Beggar's Opera* made the reluctant Mr. Rich a wealthy man. In all, the manager of the Theatre Royal cleared better than 4000 pounds from the play as compared to the author's share of 800 pounds. Respecting the play's effect on the fortunes of author and manager, a *bon mot* current at the time asserted that *The Beggar's Opera* had made "Gay rich and Rich gay"; however, as the figures cited attest, there was more poetry than truth in that assertion.

The success of *The Beggar's Opera* was such that Gay's contemporaries were convinced that the play would run forever. In a very real sense, it has done precisely that.

The play quickly became a favorite repertory piece on the London stage, and during the remainder of the eighteenth century, it was revived every year without exception until the annual revival of *The Beggar's Opera* became a fixed theatrical tradition. Nor was this popularity confined to London. Even before the original run at the Theatre Royal was over, *The Beggar's Opera* was playing the provinces (see Gay's letter of May 16, 1728) and Swift was hailing its triumphant arrival in Dublin. Moreover, the play's appeal transcended national boundaries and language barriers. In addition to performances in Scotland, Wales, and on the tiny Mediterranean island of Minorca, then a British possession, *The Beggar's Opera* was one of the first musical plays to be presented in America. In 1750 it played at the Nassau Street Theatre in New

York. It was George Washington's favorite play, and
later wrought its magic on the Puritan sensibilities of
Nathaniel Hawthorne. The cult of *The Beggar's Opera*
also caught on across the English Channel. By 1770
a French translation was available for Parisian readers,
and in Germany, Gay's opus, bearing the improbable
title *Die Strassenräuber,* was charming audiences in
Hamburg.

The vitality of *The Beggar's Opera* is a continuing
phenomenon, and its end is not yet in sight. In recent
years it has been revived in London, first in 1920
when it ran for 1463 performances, again in 1922,
1928, 1940, 1954, and most recently in 1963, under the
auspices of the Royal Shakespeare Company. *The Beggar's Opera* has appeared on Broadway as late as 1957,
and in 1953 it was translated to the motion picture
screen with no less a luminary than Sir Laurence
Olivier in the role of Macheath. Amateur productions,
especially by college dramatic groups, have been too
numerous to chronicle. With complete justification
The Beggar's Opera has been called "the play that will
never die."

Its immortality is assured in yet other ways. The
line of genealogical descent from Gay to Gilbert and
Sullivan to latter-day political satires such as *Of Thee
I Sing, Fiorello,* and *Mr. President* is particularly di-
rect, but, at the same time, it is only a slight exaggera-
tion to say that every time the curtain goes up on a
modern musical comedy, *The Beggar's Opera* is being
played again.

The Beggar's Opera lives on too by virtue of the
inspiration it has provided for a long line of dramatists
and composers throughout the years, beginning with
Johann Pepusch, a German expatriate in London like
Handel, who wrote the play's charming overture.
Through the mid-eighteenth century, a host of greater
and lesser talents tried their hands at the new genre,
the ballad opera, and, in modern times *The Beggar's
Opera* has inspired such various talents as Duke El-

lington, who wrote the score for a musical comedy entitled *The Beggar's Holiday*, and Bertolt Brecht and Kurt Weil, who, in collaborating on an updated version of the two-centuries-old play, produced a classic in its own right, *The Three Penny Opera*. And it was through the unwitting efforts of Brecht and Weil that *The Beggar's Opera*'s fame reached an unlikely zenith in the early 1960's when "Mack the Knife," a popular rendition of one of the melodies from *The Three Penny Opera*, became Number One on the Hit Parade and made Macheath, Suky Tawdry, and Jenny Diver household names.

The key word in accounting for *The Beggar's Opera*'s extraordinary appeal for the audiences of Gay's time is novelty. The touch of originality can best be seen in Gay's handling of the literary, social, and political satire in the play.

Although part of the attack was directed at sentimental comedy, the chief target of the literary satire in *The Beggar's Opera* was the Italian Opera, then the reigning favorite on the London stage. For audiences accustomed to the formal, stylized Italian Opera sung in a language that few theatregoers understood, Gay's noisy and fast-moving musical play, utilizing traditional ballads with which they had been familiar since childhood and spoken and sung entirely in English, was, indeed, a distinct and refreshing novelty.

The use of familiar ballads served Gay in a number of ways. In contrast to the extravagance and pretense of the Italian arias, Gay's airs were characterized by the simplest of melodies and the homeliest diction. They were, in other words, songs that were native to the English spirit and temperament, and their employment provoked Gay's audiences to consider the basic incongruity of foreign-language opera on the English stage. The incongruity was underscored by the setting Gay provided for his ballad airs. Such charming and beloved melodies as "Greensleeves" or the catchy "Britons Strike Home" were clearly out of place in the boisterous and squalid atmosphere of Newgate Prison—but no more so, was the implicit commentary, than Italian arias at Drury Lane.

In using traditional ballads and folk airs, Gay occasionally introduced a satiric twist that further enhanced the novelty of *The Beggar's Opera*. For each of the ballads Gay wrote new lyrics, and in several instances he purposely supplied rollicking, rowdy lyrics for airs which, in their original forms, had been fine, old, sentimental melodies. The nostalgic air, "The bonny grey-ey'd morn," for example, was transformed into the cynical ditty, " 'Tis woman that seduces all mankind" (Air II), sung by Filch, the pickpocket. Similarly, the opening line of the stirring favorite, "Oh London is a fine town," became the raucous, "Our Polly is a sad slut" (Air VII). In Act III Lucy Lockit, a kind of lyrical Lucrezia Borgia, attempts to cajole Polly into drinking a cordial heavily laced with ratsbane by singing the air, "Come, sweet lass/Let's take a chirping glass." Lucy's air is based on the popular old ballad, with its strong pastoral overtones, "Come, sweet lass/This bonny weather." The shock of recognition which came to Gay's audiences on hearing these traditional favorites in their new mountings must have been startling. So too, the attempt to reconcile sentimental associations usually conjured up by the melodies they were hearing with the comic response demanded by Gay's lyrics must have delighted and intrigued the audience.

One final facet of the literary satire deserves consideration. Not least among the many firsts associated with *The Beggar's Opera* is the fact that it was the first musical play on the English stage in which songs and story are integrated. In *The Beggar's Opera*, the airs are prompted by the dramatic situations, and, at the same time, they further the action of the plot. By accompanying his play with music that was something more than incidental, Gay served at once the ends of novelty and literary satire. By 1728 the vogue of the individual performer (the leading tenor or the prima donna) had caught on so in the Italian Opera that many of the arias were completely divorced from the plot. They were introduced, in fact, to display the virtuosity of the current favorite and had the effect of halting the action for the sake of a musical digression (see Gay's letter of February 3, 1723). Thus, Gay's careful blending of book and music was not only fresh and new but it also pointed up the absurdity of the Italian Opera's practice.

For much of the social satire in *The Beggar's Opera* Gay drew upon his own experiences during his fourteen-year pursuit of a place at Court, a luckless, frustrating, and, finally, humiliating odyssey that resulted only in promises unkept and hopes unfulfilled (see *Epistle to a Lady, The Hare and Many Friends,* and several of Gay's letters). It should be recalled that this was an age when patronage was a way of life, when all artists and writers were subsidized by the affluent, the influential, or, by the Court. (Gay's friend Pope was the first writer in the long history of English literature to support himself solely from his work, the first professional writer in the fullest sense of the word). In seeking a sinecure at Court, Gay was asking no more than what was thought at the time to be his due.

In 1727 on the accession of George II to the throne, Gay was offered the menial post of Gentleman-Usher to the two-year-old Princess Louisa. In view of his careful cultivation of the new Queen Caroline (dating back to 1714), rightly or wrongly Gay evidently expected something better. Feeling cheated and insulted, he refused the appointment and was convinced that hypocrisy and double dealing constituted the accepted code at St. James's Palace and Whitehall. He was convinced too that the English public should share his new-found disenchantment. How to expose this moral bankruptcy in high places was a difficult problem, however, since peculation was often disguised as political necessity, or even patriotism, and dissembling had acquired the deceptive veneer of genteel manners and proper diction. In his search for a means of penetrating this surface covering of respectability, Gay recalled the three highwaymen, Jonathan Wild, Jack Sheppard, and Jonathan Blake, whose trial at the Old Bailey in 1725 he had celebrated in his poem, "Newgate's Garland." Wild, in betraying his erstwhile comrades, demonstrated convincingly the validity of the old adage that there is no honor among thieves. Gay had found little honor at the opposite end of the social scale among the "great" of the world. Minister and malefactor, cutpurse and courtier were blood brothers morally. The solution to the problem, then, lay in the novel device of interchanging the two worlds, Newgate and the Hanoverian Court, and displaying their consanguinity.

Throughout *The Beggar's Opera*, Gay's footpads, cutthroats, and pickpockets and their unseemly consorts, the streetwalkers of Drury Lane, ape the manners and adopt the attitudes of their betters. In Act II, Scene V, for instance, Macheath's "ladies" observe an elaborate and, for them, preposterous courtesy in their conversational exchanges, Peachum and Lockit insist that they are honorable men of affairs, and Macheath unfailingly addresses the members of his gang as "gentlemen." Thus, the message was translated into visual terms, and even the most unobservant in Gay's audiences could see that despite the protective coloring he wears and the air of gentility he assumes, a knave is still a knave.

The text of the lesson Gay was preaching is set forth in the opening lines of the play with the boisterous air, "Through all the employments of life." Though Gay makes passing thrusts at the lawyers and divines, the fundamental burden of this air is to establish the kinship between Peachum, the evil genius of the Newgate community, and his counterpart at Whitehall, the "great" statesman. Lest the audience become captivated by his raffish cast of characters and lose sight of the parable being developed, Gay returned to the charge again and again. The terms "tribe" and "gang" are used indiscriminately in reference to highwaymen and courtiers, Mrs. Peachum is punctilious in adhering to the practice of the *haut monde* by drinking strong waters only in private, and in an explicit statement of the play's social philosophy, the Beggar observes that it is difficult to determine whether "the fine gentlemen imitate the gentlemen of the road, or the gentlemen of the road the fine gentlemen." Armed with these clues, the audiences which filled the Theatre Royal nightly during that first season had no difficulty recognizing that the people on the stage, much like the figures in medieval allegory, stood for something else —that for "Newgate," one should read "Whitehall."

The appearance of *The Beggar's Opera* in 1728 provided a central chapter in the history of English political satire. It was the single most effective attack launched by the Tories against the Whig Ministry under the second George, and literary historians are in general agreement that the play was the first step in an inexorable sequence of events which culminated in the closing of the theatres and the Licensing Act of 1737. Herein lies an exquisite irony.

In one of his earliest published works, *The Present State of Wit*, Gay wrote that he cared not "one farthing for Whig or Tory," and his later career testifies to the validity of that assertion. In an era of strong party allegiances, his apathy toward political matters was remarkable. Gay was a Tory simply because his friends Swift and Pope were Tories. He was, therefore, the least likely candidate for the role of Tory advocate which fell to him as a result of *The Beggar's Opera*. Thus, it is probably safe to say that personal pique rather than party conviction motivated the political satire in the play.

In his disappointment over failing to win a significant place at Court, Gay was disposed to listen to his Tory companions, who persuaded him that the rebuff was politically inspired. As a result, Gay fixed upon the Whig Prime Minister, Robert Walpole, as the architect of all his woes.

The principal attack on Walpole is carried out through Gay's characterization of the despicable Peachum, the Prime Minister's alter ego in the play. In accord with Gay's view of Peachum's counterpart at Whitehall, Peachum is the chief villain of the piece. In the world of Newgate, Peachum is the master manipulator, a thoroughgoing cynic, and, above all, a man with his eyes firmly fixed on the main chance for turning a profit. Thus, Walpole, in Gay's opinion, was the Peachum of the world of Whitehall.

In Peachum's *weltanschauung*, money is basic; it is his firm conviction that hard cash (and not love) makes the world go 'round. Peachum's preoccupation with the power of the pound sterling hit at Walpole in two ways. It reflected the widely-held contemporary belief that Walpole had used his office to amass a vast personal fortune. At the same time, Peachum's faith in the well-placed perquisite mirrored Walpole's celebrated political *modus operandi*, "Every man has his price."

In exposing Walpole's materialism, however, Gay was only warming to the attack. Among his many lucrative albeit unlawful pursuits, Peachum is, as his name implies, an informer, who betrays his companions for the sake of the reward offered for their apprehension. Like his prototype, Jonathan Wild, Peachum realizes a dual profit from his association with London's criminal set. He profits in his capacity as a fence and he profits from the capture of his underlings when they have ceased to be of service to him. The whole sordid business is reminiscent, as Gay intended it should be, of Walpole's alleged sangfroid in using people to further his own ends. The satire, moreover, reached devastating proportions when Gay's audiences realized that, through Peachum, he was linking Walpole not only with the criminal element generally but specifically with the pariah Wild, perhaps the most odious villain ever to ride the carts to Tyburn.

The Beggar's Opera was not the first Tory attack on Walpole and the Whig Ministry, but it was the one that struck home. Its effectiveness can be understood by referring again to novelty and originality.

Much of the Tory effort at political satire was heavy-handed and uninspired—conventional pamphlets addressed to the party faithful and mechanically produced by hack writers whose notions of subtlety lay in disguising the target as "W-lp-le, the Pr-me M-n-st-r." This ineffectual badgering bothered Walpole not one whit. He was intelligent enough to realize that he had nothing to fear from such puerility.

The Beggar's Opera succeeded in unsettling Walpole's composure precisely because it was something more than the conventional political document. The play was, above all else, entertaining, which the stock pamphlets were not. Gay was careful to amuse his audience while indoctrinating them politically. In addition, *The Beggar's Opera* reached a large and diversified audience. For a few pennies the meanest apprentice in London could occupy a seat in the gallery at the Theatre Royal and witness the nightly spectacle of the King's government and its chief minister being reduced to a comic shambles. This was something that Walpole could not and did not tolerate for long. A year later when Gay sought to bring *Polly*, sequel to *The Beggar's Opera*, to the stage, the play was summarily suppressed.

Novelty also plays a role in accounting for *The Beggar's Opera*'s appeal to modern audiences. For the twentieth-century viewer (or reader), the play has an old-fashioned quaintness and measured charm that is in refreshing contrast to the strident choruses of to-day's neon-lighted Broadway musicals. Ultimately, in endeavoring to pinpoint the source of *The Beggar's Opera*'s longevity, one can only refer to the quality best described, however unsatisfactorily, as "magic"— the power to strike an instant rapport with an audience, to reach across the footlights and engage the audience and make them a part of the never-never world being brought to life on the stage. This magic *The Beggar's Opera* has, and after two hundred and thirty-eight years it shows no signs of losing its potency.

The text of *The Beggar's Opera* was transcribed from the Yale Library's copy of the third edition of the play published in 1729, the latest edition Gay is known to have corrected. The texts of the companion pieces are from various early editions of these works among the holdings of the Harvard Library. The excerpts from Gay's letters are from the originals. Some effort has been made to preserve the distinctive eighteenth-century spellings and printing practices. Whenever the eighteenth-century forms would result in difficulties in reading, however, the text has been modernized.

PRINCIPAL DATES IN THE LIFE
OF JOHN GAY

1685 John Gay born June 30 at Barnstaple to a prominent Devonshire family. Educated at the Barnstaple Grammar School.

1702 Apprentice to a silk merchant in London until 1706; apprenticeship ends by mutual agreement and Gay returns briefly to Barnstaple.

1707 Again in London as secretary to former Barnstaple schoolmate, the dramatist Aaron Hill, who introduces him to London literary circles.

1708 Begins literary career with burlesque poem, *Wine*.

1711 Meets Pope, Addison, Congreve, Arbuthnot.

1712 First play, *The Mohocks*, written but not produced. Domestic steward until 1714 to the Duchess of Monmouth, widow of Charles II's illegitimate son, the "Absalom" of Dryden's *Absalom and Achitophel*.

1713 Publishes two poems, *Rural Sports* and *The Fan*. His play *The Wife of Bath* produced at Drury Lane.

1714 Writes first real success, *The Shepherd's Week*. Member of Scriblerus Club with Pope, Swift, Arbuthnot, Parnell, and Oxford. Goes to Hanover in Germany as secretary to the Clarendon Mission. Meets the future Queen Caroline.

1715 *The What D'ye Call It*, a "Tragi-Comi-Pastoral Farce," has successful run at Drury Lane. Gay living in London, cultivating literary acquaintances and friends at Court.

1716 *Trivia*, an artistic and financial success. Collaborates with Pope and Arbuthnot on unsuccessful farce, *Three Hours After Marriage*.

1720 Publishes *Poems on Several Occasions*, a collection of miscellaneous works. Loses heavily in the South Sea Bubble.

1723   Made Commissioner of the State Lottery. Occupies apartment at Whitehall.

1724   *The Captives,* a tragedy, produced at Drury Lane.

1726   Swift in England. Lives with Gay at Whitehall. Pope, Swift, and Gay spend summer months at Twickenham. Gay at work on the *Fables*.

1727   The *Fables,* Volume I, published. Gay rejects Court appointment as Gentleman-Usher to Princess Louisa.

1728   *The Beggar's Opera* premieres January 29 and runs for a record sixty-two performances.

1729   *Polly,* sequel to *The Beggar's Opera,* banned from the stage. Gay joins the Duke and Duchess of Queensberry in voluntary exile from the Court.

1731   *Acis and Galatea,* a pastoral opera.

1732   Gay dies December 4. Buried in the Poets' Corner in Westminster Abbey near Chaucer.

THE BEGGAR'S OPERA

*Nos hæc novimus esse nihil.**

---

* We know these things to be nothing at all. Martial.

THE BEGGAR'S OPERA

DRAMATIS PERSONAE

PEACHUM
LOCKIT
MACHEATH
FILCH
JEMMY TWITCHER ⎫
CROOK-FINGERED JACK ⎮
WAT DREARY ⎮
ROBIN OF BAGSHOT ⎮
NIMMING NED ⎬ *Macheath's gang*
HARRY PADINGTON ⎮
MATT OF THE MINT ⎮
BEN BUDGE ⎭
BEGGAR
PLAYER

Constables, Drawer, Turnkey

MRS. PEACHUM
POLLY PEACHUM
LUCY LOCKIT
DIANA TRAPES
MRS. COAXER ⎫
DOLLY TRULL ⎮
MRS. VIXEN ⎮
BETTY DOXY ⎮
JENNY DIVER ⎬ *Women of the town*
MRS. SLAMMEKIN ⎮
SUKY TAWDRY ⎮
MOLLY BRAZEN ⎭

INTRODUCTION

BEGGAR, PLAYER

BEGGAR. If poverty be a title to poetry, I am sure no-body can dispute mine. I own myself of the company of beggars; and I make one at their weekly festivals at St. Giles's.[2] I have a small yearly salary for my catches,[3] and am welcome to a dinner there whenever I please, which is more than most poets can say.

PLAYER. As we live by the Muses, 'tis but gratitude in us to encourage poetical merit where-ever we find it. The Muses, contrary to all other ladies, pay no distinction to dress, and never partially[4] mistake the pertness of embroidery for wit, nor the modesty of want for dulness. Be the author who he will, we push his play as far as it will go. So (though you are in want) I wish you success heartily.

BEGGAR. This piece I own was originally writ for the celebrating the marriage of James Chanter and Moll Lay, two most excellent ballad-singers. I have introduc'd the similes that are in all your celebrated operas: the Swallow, the Moth, the Bee, the Ship, the Flower, etc. Besides, I have a prison scene, which the ladies always reckon charmingly pathetick. As to the parts, I have observ'd such a nice impartiality to our two ladies, that it is impossible for either of them to take offence.[5] I hope I may be forgiven, that I have not made my opera throughout unnatural, like those in vogue; for I have no recitative: excepting this, as I

[2] **St. Giles's** the district around St. Giles's in the Fields was London's skid row in the early eighteenth century   [3] **catches** popular songs, often burlesque and often obscene   [4] **partially** being partial   [5] An allusion to a contemporary quarrel between the two leading sopranos of the Italian Opera

have consented to have neither prologue nor epilogue, it must be allow'd an opera in all its forms. The piece indeed hath been heretofore frequently represented by ourselves in our great room at St. Giles's, so that I cannot too often acknowledge your charity in bringing it now on the stage.

PLAYER. But I see 'tis time for us to withdraw; the actors are preparing to begin. Play away the ouverture.

(*Exeunt*)

THE BEGGAR'S OPERA

❧

Act I

SCENE I

PEACHUM'S *House*

(PEACHUM *sitting at a table with a large book of accounts before him*)

AIR I. *An old woman cloathed in gray.*[1]

Through all the employments of life
Each neighbour abuses his brother;
Whore and rogue they call husband and wife:
All professions be-rogue one another.
The priest calls the lawyer a cheat,
The lawyer be-knaves the divine;
And the statesman, because he's so great,[2]
Thinks his trade as honest as mine.

A lawyer is an honest employment, so is mine. Like me too he acts in a double capacity, both against rogues and for 'em; for 'tis but fitting that we should protect and encourage cheats, since we live by 'em.

SCENE II

PEACHUM, FILCH

FILCH. Sir, Black Moll hath sent word her tryal comes on in the afternoon, and she hopes you will order matters so as to bring her off.

[1] For the music of *The Beggar's Opera,* Gay employed familiar ballads for which he wrote new lyrics. The ballad source, if known, will be given at the beginning of each air [2] **great a** term often applied to Walpole with sarcastic overtones

PEACHUM. Why, she may plead her belly at worst;[1] to my knowledge she hath taken care of that security. But as the wench is very active and industrious, you may satisfy her that I'll soften the evidence.

FILCH. Tom Gagg, Sir, is found guilty.

PEACHUM. A lazy dog! When I took him the time before, I told him what he would come to if he did not mend his hand. This is death without reprieve. I may venture to book him. (*Writes*) For Tom Gagg, forty pounds. Let Betty Sly know that I'll save her from transportation,[2] for I can get more by her staying in England.

FILCH. Betty hath brought more goods into our lock[3] to-year than any five of the gang; and in truth, 'tis a pity to lose so good a customer.

PEACHUM. If none of the gang take her off, she may, in the common course of business, live a twelve-month longer. I love to let women scape. A good sportsman always lets the hen-partridges fly, because the breed of the game depends upon them. Besides, here the law allows us no reward; there is nothing to be got by the death of women—except our wives.

FILCH. Without dispute, she is a fine woman! 'Twas to her I was oblig'd for my education, and (to say a bold word) she hath train'd up more young fellows to the business than the gaming-table.

PEACHUM. Truly, Filch, thy observation is right. We and the surgeons are more beholden to women than all the professions besides.

AIR II. *The bonny grey-ey'd morn, etc.*

FILCH. 'Tis woman that seduces all mankind,
    By her we first were taught the wheedling arts:
    Her very eyes can cheat; when most she's kind,
    She tricks us of our money with our hearts.
    For her, like wolves by night we roam for prey,

[1] **plead her belly** by law, pregnant women could not be hanged
[2] **transportation** criminals were frequently sent to work, virtually as slaves, in the colonies   [3] **lock** warehouse for stolen goods

And practise ev'ry fraud to bribe her charms;
For suits of love, like law, are won by pay,
And beauty must be fee'd into our arms.

PEACHUM. But make haste to Newgate,[4] boy, and
let my friends know what I intend; for I love to make
them easy one way or other.

FILCH. When a gentleman is long kept in suspence,
penitence may break his spirit ever after. Besides, cer-
tainty gives a man a good air upon his tryal, and
makes him risque another without fear or scruple. But
I'll away, for 'tis a pleasure to be the messenger of
comfort to friends in affliction.

SCENE III

PEACHUM

But 'tis now high time to look about me for a decent
execution against next Sessions.[1] I hate a lazy rogue,
by whom one can get nothing 'till he is hang'd. A regis-
ter of the gang. (*reading*) Crook-finger'd Jack. A year
and a half in the service; let me see how much the
stock owes to his industry; one, two, three, four, five
gold watches, and seven silver ones. A mighty clean-
handed fellow! Sixteen snuff-boxes, five of them of
true gold. Six dozen of handkerchiefs, four silver-
hilted swords, half a dozen of shirts, three tye-perri-
wigs, and a piece of broad cloth. Considering these
are only the fruits of his leisure hours, I don't know a
prettier fellow, for no man alive hath a more engaging
presence of mind upon the road.[2] Wat Dreary, alias
Brown Will, an irregular dog, who hath an underhand
way of disposing of his goods. I'll try him only for a
Sessions or two longer upon his good behavior. Harry
Padington, a poor petty-larceny rascal, without the

[4] **Newgate** London's most notorious prison
[1] **Sessions** quarterly sessions of the criminal court. Peachum betrays his "employees" to the law when they have ceased to be
useful as thieves   [2] **upon the road** as a highwayman

least genius; that fellow, though he were to live these six months, will never come to the gallows with any credit. Slippery Sam; he goes off the next Sessions, for the villain hath the impudence to have views of following his trade as a taylor, which he calls an honest employment. Matt of the Mint; listed not above a month ago, a promising sturdy fellow, and diligent in his way; somewhat too bold and hasty, and may raise good contributions on the publick, if he does not cut himself short by murder. Tom Tipple, a guzzling soaking sot, who is always too drunk to stand himself, or to make others stand. A cart[3] is absolutely necessary for him. Robin of Bagshot,[4] alias Gorgon, alias Bluff Bob, alias Carbuncle, alias Bob Booty.

Scene IV

Peachum, Mrs. Peachum

Mrs. Peachum. What of Bob Booty, husband? I hope nothing bad hath betided him. You know, my dear, he's a favourite customer of mine. 'Twas he made me a present of this ring.

Peachum. I have set his name down in the blacklist, that's all, my dear; he spends his life among women, and as soon as his money is gone, one or other of the ladies will hang him for the reward, and there's forty pounds lost to us for-ever.

Mrs. Peachum. You know, my dear, I never meddle in matters of death; I always leave those affairs to you. Women indeed are bitter bad judges in these cases, for they are so partial to the brave that they think every man handsome who is going to the camp or the gallows.

---

[3] **cart** the cart which carried convicted felons to Tyburn Hill to be hanged   [4] **Robin of Bagshot** Bagshot Heath, just outside London, was a favorite spot for robberies

AIR III. *Cold and raw, etc.*

If any wench Venus's girdle wear,
Though she be never so ugly;
Lillies and roses will quickly appear,
And her face look wond'rous smuggly.
Beneath the left ear so fit but a cord,
(A rope so charming a zone is!)
The youth in his cart hath the air of a lord,
And we cry, there dies an Adonis!

But really, husband, you should not be too hard-hearted, for you never had a finer, braver set of men than at present. We have not had a murder among them all, these seven months. And truly, my dear, that is a great blessing.

PEACHUM. What a dickens is the woman always a whimpring about murder for? No gentleman is ever look'd upon the worse for killing a man in his own defence; and if business cannot be carried on without it, what would you have a gentleman do?

MRS. PEACHUM. If I am in the wrong, my dear, you must excuse me, for no-body can help the frailty of an overscrupulous conscience.

PEACHUM. Murder is as fashionable a crime as a man can be guilty of. How many fine gentlemen have we in Newgate every year, purely upon that article! If they have wherewithal to persuade the jury to bring it in manslaughter, what are they the worse for it? So, my dear, have done upon this subject. Was Captain Macheath here this morning, for the bank-notes he left with you last week?

MRS. PEACHUM. Yes, my dear; and though the bank hath stopt payment, he was so cheerful and so agreeable! sure there is not a finer gentleman upon the road than the captain! If he comes from Bagshot at any reasonable hour he hath promis'd to make one this evening with Polly and me, and Bob Booty, at a party of quadrille.[1] Pray, my dear, is the captain rich?

PEACHUM. The captain keeps too good company ever to grow rich. Marybone[2] and the chocolate-houses are his undoing. The man that proposes to get money by play should have the education of a fine gentleman, and be train'd up to it from his youth.

MRS. PEACHUM. Really, I am sorry upon Polly's account the captain hath not more discretion. What business hath he to keep company with lords and gentlemen? he should leave them to prey upon one another.

PEACHUM. Upon Polly's account! What, a plague, does the woman mean?—Upon Polly's account!

MRS. PEACHUM. Captain Macheath is very fond of the girl.

PEACHUM. And what then?

MRS. PEACHUM. If I have any skill in the ways of women, I am sure Polly thinks him a very pretty man.

PEACHUM. And what then? You would not be so mad to have the wench marry him! Gamesters and highwaymen are generally very good to their whores, but they are very devils to their wives.

MRS. PEACHUM. But if Polly should be in love, how should we help her, or how can she help herself? Poor girl, I am in the utmost concern about her.

AIR IV. *Why is your faithful slave disdain'd?*

If love the virgin's heart invade,
How, like a moth, the simple maid
Still plays about the flame!
If soon she be not made a wife,
Her honour's sing'd, and then for life,
She's—what I dare not name.

PEACHUM. Look ye, wife. A handsome wench in our

---

[1] **quadrille** a popular card game   [2] **Marybone** Marylebone, a village two miles northwest of London, whose gardens and bowling greens were a popular rendezvous for the city's gamblers and thieves

way of business is as profitable as at the bar of a Temple[3] coffee-house, who looks upon it as her livelihood to grant every liberty but one. You see I would indulge the girl as far as prudently we can. In any thing, but marriage! After that, my dear, how shall we be safe? Are we not then in her husband's power? For a husband hath the absolute power over all a wife's secrets but her own. If the girl had the discretion of a court lady, who can have a dozen young fellows at her ear without complying with one, I should not matter it; but Polly is tinder, and a spark will at once set her on a flame. Married! If the wench does not know her own profit, sure she knows her own pleasure better than to make herself a property! My daughter to me should be, like a court lady to a minister of state, a key to the whole gang.[4] Married! If the affair is not already done, I'll terrify her from it, by the example of our neighbours.

MRS. PEACHUM. May-hap, my dear, you may injure the girl. She loves to imitate the fine ladies, and she may only allow the captain liberties in the view of interest.

PEACHUM. But 'tis your duty, my dear, to warn the girl against her ruin, and to instruct her how to make the most of her beauty. I'll go to her this moment, and sift her.[5] In the meantime, wife, rip out the coronets and marks of these dozen of cambric handkerchiefs, for I can dispose of them this afternoon to a chap[6] in the city.

[3] **Temple** district between Fleet St. and the Thames where two of the Inns of Court (law schools), Inner and Middle Temple, are located [4] The use of the word "gang" furthers the parallel between high and low life, *i.e.*, gang of courtiers, or of thieves. See also Act II, i   [5] **sift her** sound her out   [6] **chap** customer

Scene V

Mrs. Peachum

Never was a man more out of the way in an argument than my husband! Why must our Polly, forsooth, differ from her sex, and love only her husband? And why must Polly's marriage, contrary to all observation, make her the less followed by other men? All men are thieves in love, and like a woman the better for being another's property.

AIR V. *Of all the simple things we do, etc.*

A maid is like the golden ore,
Which hath guineas intrinsical in't,
Whose worth is never known, before
It is try'd and imprest in the Mint.
A wife's like a guinea in gold,
Stampt with the name of her spouse;
Now here, now there; is bought, or is sold;
And is current in every house.

Scene VI

Mrs. Peachum, Filch

MRS. PEACHUM. Come hither Filch. I am as fond of this child, as though my mind misgave me he were my own. He hath as fine a hand at picking a pocket as a woman, and is as nimble-finger'd as a juggler. If an unlucky Session does not cut the rope of thy life, I pronounce, boy, thou wilt be a great man in history. Where was your post last night, my boy?

FILCH. I ply'd at the opera, madam; and considering 'twas neither dark nor rainy, so that there was no great hurry in getting chairs and coaches, made a tolerable hand on't. These seven handkerchiefs, madam.

MRS. PEACHUM. Colour'd ones, I see. They are of

sure sale from our ware-house at Redriff [1] among the seamen.

FILCH. And this snuff-box.

MRS. PEACHUM. Set in gold! A pretty encouragement this to a young beginner.

FILCH. I had a fair tug at a charming gold watch. Pox take the taylors for making the fobs so deep and narrow! It stuck by the way, and I was forc'd to make my escape under a coach. Really, madam, I fear I shall be cut off in the flower of my youth, so that every now and then (since I was pumpt) [2] I have thoughts of taking up and going to sea.

MRS. PEACHUM. You should go to Hockley in the Hole, [3] and to Marybone, child, to learn valour. These are the schools that have bred so many brave men. I thought, boy, by this time, thou hadst lost fear as well as shame. Poor lad! how little does he know as yet of the Old-Baily! [4] For the first fact, I'll insure thee from being hang'd; and going to sea, Filch, will come time enough upon a sentence of transportation. But now, since you have nothing better to do, ev'n go to your book, and learn your catechism; for really a man makes but an ill figure in the ordinary's paper, [5] who cannot give a satisfactory answer to his questions. But, hark you, my lad. Don't tell me a lye; for you know I hate a lyar. Do you know of any thing that hath past between Captain Macheath and our Polly?

FILCH. I beg you, madam, don't ask me; for I must either tell a lye to you or to Miss Polly; for I promis'd her I would not tell.

MRS. PEACHUM. But when the honour of our family is concern'd—

FILCH. I shall lead a sad life with Miss Polly, if ever

---

[1] **Redriff** dock section of London   [2] **pumpt** held under the public pump, a punishment for juvenile offenders   [3] **Hockley in the Hole** where bear-baiting and other violent entertainments were held   [4] **Old-Baily** (Old Bailey), London's central criminal court   [5] **ordinary's paper** the prison chaplain's report of a condemned man's confession

she come to know that I told you. Besides, I would not willingly forfeit my own honour by betraying any body.

MRS. PEACHUM. Yonder comes my husband and Polly. Come, Filch, you shall go with me into my own room, and tell me the whole story. I'll give thee a most delicious glass of a cordial [6] that I keep for my own drinking.

SCENE VII

PEACHUM, POLLY

POLLY. I know as well as any of the fine ladies how to make the most of my self and of my man too. A woman knows how to be mercenary, though she hath never been in a court or at an assembly.[1] We have it in our natures, papa. If I allow Captain Macheath some trifling liberties, I have this watch and other visible marks of his favour to show for it. A girl who cannot grant some things, and refuse what is most material, will make but a poor hand of her beauty, and soon be thrown upon the common.

AIR VI. *What shall I do to show how much I love her?*

> Virgins are like the fair flower in its lustre,
> Which in the garden enamels the ground;
> Near it the bees in play flutter and cluster,
> And gaudy butterflies frolick around.
> But, when once pluck'd, 'tis no longer alluring,
> To Covent-Garden[2] 'tis sent, (as yet sweet,)
> There fades, and shrinks, and grows past all enduring,
> Rots, stinks, and dies, and is trod under feet.

PEACHUM. You know, Polly, I am not against your toying and trifling with a customer in the way of

[6] cordial a liqueur
[1] assembly social gathering or ball   [2] Covent-Garden London's chief flower market. Because it was also the haunt of prostitutes in Gay's time, there are a number of *double entendres* in the passage

business, or to get out a secret or so. But if I find
out that you have play'd the fool and are married, you
jade you, I'll cut your throat, hussy. Now you know
my mind.

Scene VIII

Peachum, Polly, Mrs. Peachum

Air VII. *Oh London is a fine town.*

(Mrs. Peachum, *in a very great passion*)

Our Polly is a sad slut! nor heeds what we have
    taught her.
I wonder any man alive will ever rear a daughter!
For she must have both hoods and gowns, and hoops
    to swell her pride.
With scarfs, and stays, and gloves and lace; and
    she will have men beside;
And when she's drest with care and cost, all-tempting,
    fine and gay,
As men should serve a cowcumber,[1] she flings her-
    self away.

You baggage! you hussy! you inconsiderate jade! had
you been hang'd, it would not have vex'd me, for that
might have been your misfortune; but to do such a
mad thing by choice! The wench is married, husband.

Peachum. Married! The captain is a bold man, and
will risque any thing for money; to be sure he believes
her a fortune. Do you think your mother and I should
have liv'd comfortably so long together, if ever we had
been married? Baggage!

Mrs. Peachum. I knew she was always a proud slut;
and now the wench hath play'd the fool and married,
because forsooth she would do like the gentry. Can
you support the expence of a husband, hussy, in gaming, drinking and whoring? have you money enough
to carry on the daily quarrels of man and wife about
who shall squander most? There are not many hus-

---

[1] **cowcumber** cucumber

bands and wives, who can bear the charges of plaguing one another in a handsome way, If you must be married, could you introduce no-body into our family but a highwayman? Why, thou foolish jade, thou wilt be as ill-us'd, and as much neglected, as if thou hadst married a lord!

PEACHUM. Let not your anger, my dear, break through the rules of decency, for the captain looks upon himself in the military capacity, as a gentleman by his profession. Besides what he hath already, I know he is in a fair way of getting, or of dying; and both these ways, let me tell you, are most excellent chances for a wife.[2] Tell me, hussy, are you ruin'd or no?

MRS. PEACHUM. With Polly's fortune, she might very well have gone off to a person of distinction. Yes, that you might, you pouting slut!

PEACHUM. What, is the wench dumb? Speak, or I'll make you plead by squeezing out an answer from you. Are you really bound wife to him, or are you only upon liking?

(*Pinches her*)

POLLY. Oh! (*Screaming*)

MRS. PEACHUM. How the mother is to be pitied who hath handsome daughters! Locks, bolts, bars, and lectures of morality are nothing to them: they break through them all. They have as much pleasure in cheating a father and mother, as in cheating at cards.

PEACHUM. Why, Polly, I shall soon know if you are married, by Macheath's keeping from our house.

AIR VIII. *Grim king of the ghosts, etc.*

POLLY. Can love be controul'd by advice?
Will Cupid our mothers obey?

---

[2] This scene is a broad take-off on a stock situation in eighteenth-century stage comedy—the dutiful child torn between the demands of her heart and her parents' insistence on a marriage of convenience

Though my heart were as frozen as ice,
At his flame 'twould have melted away.

When he kist me so closely he prest,
'Twas so sweet that I must have comply'd:
So I thought it both safest and best
To marry, for fear you should chide.

MRS. PEACHUM. Then all the hopes of our family are gone for ever and ever!

PEACHUM. And Macheath may hang his father and mother-in-law, in hope to get into their daughter's fortune.

POLLY. I did not marry him (as 'tis the fashion) cooly and deliberately for honour or money. But, I love him.

MRS. PEACHUM. Love him! worse and worse! I thought the girl had been better bred. Oh husband, husband! her folly makes me mad! my head swims! I'm distracted! I can't support myself—Oh! (*Faints*)

PEACHUM. See, wench, to what a condition you have reduc'd your poor mother! a glass of cordial, this instant. How the poor woman takes it to heart! (POLLY *goes out and returns with it*) Ah, hussy, now this is the only comfort your mother has left!

POLLY. Give her another glass, sir; my mama drinks double the quantity whenever she is out of order. This, you see, fetches[3] her.

MRS. PEACHUM. The girl shows such a readiness, and so much concern, that I could almost find it in my heart to forgive her.

AIR IX. *O Jenny, O Jenny, where hast thou been.*

O Polly, you might have toy'd and kist.
By keeping men off, you keep them on.
POLLY. But he so teaz'd me,
And he so pleas'd me,
What I did, you must have done.

[3] fetches revives

MRS. PEACHUM. Not with a highwayman.—You sorry slut!

PEACHUM. A word with you, wife. 'Tis no new thing for a wench to take man without consent of parents. You know 'tis the frailty of woman, my dear.

MRS. PEACHUM. Yes, indeed, the sex is frail. But the first time a woman is frail, she should be somewhat nice[4] methinks, for then or never is the time to make her fortune. After that, she hath nothing to do but to guard herself from being found out, and she may do what she pleases.

PEACHUM. Make your self a little easy; I have a thought shall soon set all matters again to rights. Why so melancholy, Polly? since what is done cannot be undone, we must all endeavour to make the best of it.

MRS. PEACHUM. Well, Polly; as far as one woman can forgive another, I forgive thee.—Your father is too fond of you, hussy.

POLLY. Then all my sorrows are at an end.

MRS. PEACHUM. A mighty likely speech in troth, for a wench who is just married!

AIR X. *Thomas, I cannot, etc.*

POLLY. I, like a ship in storms, was tost;
    Yet afraid to put in to land;
    For seiz'd in the port the vessel's lost,
    Whose treasure is contreband.
    The waves are laid,
    My duty's paid.
    O joy beyond expression!
    Thus, safe a-shore,
    I ask no more,
    My all is in my possession.

PEACHUM. I hear customers in t'other room; go, talk with 'em, Polly; but come to us again, as soon as they are gone.—But, hark ye, child, if 'tis the gentleman

[4] nice careful, discriminating

who was here yesterday about the repeating-watch;[5] say, you believe we can't get intelligence of it, till to-morrow. For I lent it to Suky Straddle, to make a figure with it to-night at a tavern in Drury-Lane.[6] If t'other gentleman calls for the silver-hilted sword; you know Beetle-brow'd Jemmy hath it on, and he doth not come from Tunbridge[7] till Tuesday night; so that it cannot be had till then.

SCENE IX

PEACHUM, MRS. PEACHUM

PEACHUM. Dear wife, be a little pacified. Don't let your passion run away with your senses. Polly, I grant you, hath done a rash thing.

MRS. PEACHUM. If she had had only an intrigue with the fellow, why the very best families have excus'd and huddled up a frailty of that sort. 'Tis marriage, husband, that makes it a blemish.

PEACHUM. But money, wife, is the true fuller's earth[1] for reputations, there is not a spot or a stain but what it can take out. A rich rogue now-a-days is fit company for any gentleman; and the world, my dear, hath not such a contempt for roguery as you imagine. I tell you, wife, I can make this match turn to our advantage.

MRS. PEACHUM. I am very sensible, husband, that Captain Macheath is worth money, but I am in doubt whether he hath not two or three wives already, and

[5] repeating watch an elaborate pocket watch which struck the time [6] Drury-Lane a section near Covent Garden, famous for its theatre and infamous for its streetwalkers [7] Tunbridge New Tunbridge Wells, a fashionable spa located a few miles north of London. The "silver-hilted sword" would enable Jemmy, a pickpocket, to mingle more readily with the elegantly dressed gentry
[1] fuller's earth a claylike substance used as a purifying or cleaning agent; in the modern sense, a spot remover

then if he should dye in a Session or two, Polly's dower would come into dispute.

PEACHUM. That, indeed, is a point which ought to be consider'd.

AIR XI. *A soldier and a sailor.*

A fox may steal your hens, sir,
A whore your health and pence, sir,
Your daughter rob your chest, sir,
Your wife may steal your rest, sir,
A thief your goods and plate.[2]
But this is all but picking;
With rest, pence, chest and chicken,
It ever was decreed, sir,
If lawyer's hand is fee'd, sir,
He steals your whole estate.

The lawyers are bitter enemies to those in our way. They don't care that any body should get a clandestine livelihood but themselves.

SCENE X

MRS. PEACHUM, PEACHUM, POLLY

POLLY. 'Twas only Nimming Ned.[1] He brought in a damask window-curtain, a hoop-petticoat, a pair of silver candlesticks, a perriwig, and one silk stocking from the fire that happen'd last night.

PEACHUM. There is not a fellow that is cleverer in his way, and saves more goods out of the fire than Ned. But now, Polly, to your affair; for matters must not be left as they are. You are married then, it seems?

POLLY. Yes, sir.

PEACHUM. And how do you propose to live, child?

POLLY. Like other women, sir, upon the industry of my husband.

MRS. PEACHUM. What, is the wench turn'd fool? A

---

[2] **plate** silver or gold tableware
[1] **Nimming Ned** from "nim," to steal; thus, Thieving Ned

highwayman's wife, like a soldier's, hath as little of his pay, as of his company.

PEACHUM. And had not you the common views of a gentlewoman in your marriage, Polly?

POLLY. I don't know what you mean, sir.

PEACHUM. Of a jointure,[2] and of being a widow.

POLLY. But I love him, sir: how then could I have thoughts of parting with him?

PEACHUM. Parting with him! Why, that is the whole scheme and intention of all marriage articles. The comfortable estate of widow-hood, is the only hope that keeps up a wife's spirits. Where is the woman who would scruple to be a wife, if she had it in her power to be a widow whenever she pleas'd? If you have any views of this sort, Polly, I shall think the match not so very unreasonable.

POLLY. How I dread to hear your advice! Yet I must beg you to explain yourself.

PEACHUM. Secure what he hath got, have him peach'd[3] the next Sessions, and then at once you are made a rich widow.

POLLY. What, murder the man I love! The blood runs cold at my heart with the very thought of it.

PEACHUM. Fye, Polly! What hath murder to do in the affair? Since the thing sooner or later must happen, I dare say, the captain himself would like that we should get the reward for his death sooner than a stranger. Why, Polly, the captain knows, that as 'tis his employment to rob, so 'tis ours to take robbers; every man in his business. So that there is no malice in the case.

MRS. PEACHUM. Ay, husband, now you have nick'd the matter.[4] To have him peach'd is the only thing could ever make me forgive her.

---

[2] **jointure** an estate settled by a husband on his wife for her support in the event of his death   [3] **peach'd** impeached, betrayed for the reward money   [4] **nick'd the matter** come to the heart of the matter

AIR XII. *Now ponder well, ye parents dear.*

POLLY. Oh, ponder well! be not severe;
   So save a wretched wife!
   For on the rope that hangs my dear
   Depends poor Polly's life.[5]

MRS. PEACHUM. But your duty to your parents, hussy, obliges you to hang him. What would many a wife give for such an opportunity!

POLLY. What is a jointure, what is widow-hood to me? I know my heart. I cannot survive him.

AIR XIII. *Le printemps rappelle aux armes.*

The turtle thus with plaintive crying,
   Her lover dying,
The turtle thus with plaintive crying,
   Laments her dove.
Down she drops quite spent with sighing,
   Pair'd in death, as pair'd in love.

Thus, sir, it will happen to your poor Polly.

MRS. PEACHUM. What, is the fool in love in earnest then? I hate thee for being particular:[6] Why, wench, thou art a shame to thy very sex.

POLLY. But hear me, mother.—If you ever lov'd—

MRS. PEACHUM. Those cursed play-books she reads have been her ruin. One word more, hussy, and I shall knock your brains out, if you have any.

PEACHUM. Keep out of the way, Polly, for fear of mischief, and consider of what is propos'd to you.

MRS. PEACHUM. Away, hussy. Hang your husband, and be dutiful.

[5] The outrageous play on the words "hangs" and "depends" should not be overlooked   [6] **particular** different

Scene XI

Mrs. Peachum, Peachum

(Polly *listening*)

Mrs. Peachum. The thing, husband, must and shall be done. For the sake of intelligence[1] we must take other measures, and have him peach'd the next Session without her consent. If she will not know her duty, we know ours.

Peachum. But really, my dear, it grieves one's heart to take off a great man. When I consider his personal bravery, his fine stratagem,[2] how much we have already got by him, and how much more we may get, methinks I can't find it in my heart to have a hand in his death. I wish you could have made Polly undertake it.

Mrs. Peachum. But in a case of necessity—our own lives are in danger.

Peachum. Then, indeed, we must comply with the customs of the world, and make gratitude give way to interest.—He shall be taken off.

Mrs. Peachum. I'll undertake to manage Polly.

Peachum. And I'll prepare matters for the Old-Baily.

Scene XII

Polly

Now I'm a wretch, indeed.—Methinks I see him already in the cart, sweeter and more lovely than the nosegay in his hand!—I hear the crowd extolling his resolution and intrepidity!—What vollies of sighs are sent from the windows of Holborn,[1] that so comely a youth should be brought to disgrace!—I see him at the tree![2] The whole circle are in tears!—even butchers

---

[1] For . . . intelligence to meet this situation [2] stratagem skill in robbery
[1] Holborn slum district on the route to Tyburn [2] tree gallows

weep!—Jack Ketch[3] himself hesitates to perform his
duty, and would be glad to lose his fee, by a reprieve.
What then will become of Polly!—As yet I may inform
him of their design, and aid him in his escape.—It
shall be so.—But then he flies, absents himself, and
I bar my self from his dear dear conversation! That
too will distract me.—If he keep out of the way, my
papa and mama may in time relent, and we may be
happy.—If he stays, he is hang'd, and then he is lost
for ever!—He intended to lye conceal'd in my room,
'till the dusk of the evening: if they are abroad, I'll
this instant let him out, lest some accident should
prevent him.

(*Exit, and returns*)

Scene XIII

Polly, Macheath

Air XIV. *Pretty parrot, say, etc.*

Macheath. Pretty Polly, say,
    When I was away,
    Did your fancy never stray
    To some newer lover?
Polly. Without disguise,
    Heaving sighs,
    Doating eyes,
    My constant heart discover.
    Fondly let me loll!

Macheath. O pretty, pretty Poll.
Polly. And are *you* as fond as ever, my dear?
Macheath. Suspect my honour, my courage, suspect
any thing but my love.—May my pistols miss fire, and
my mare slip her shoulder while I am pursu'd, if I
ever forsake thee!
Polly. Nay, my dear, I have no reason to doubt you,
for I find in the romance you lent me, none of the
great heroes were ever false in love.

[3] **Jack Ketch** traditional name for the hangman

AIR XV. *Pray, fair one, be kind.*

MACHEATH. My heart was so free,
  It rov'd like the bee,
  'Till Polly my passion requited;
  I sipt each flower,
  I chang'd ev'ry hour,
  But here ev'ry flower is united.

POLLY. Were you sentenc'd to transportation, sure, my dear, you could not leave me behind you—could you?

MACHEATH. Is there any power, any force that could tear me from thee? You might sooner tear a pension out of the hands of a courtier, a fee from a lawyer, a pretty woman from a looking-glass, or any woman from quadrille.—But to tear me from thee is impossible!

AIR XVI. *Over the hills and far away.*

Were I laid on Greenland's coast,
  And in my arms embrac'd my lass;
Warm amidst eternal frost,
  Too soon the half year's night would pass.
POLLY. Were I sold on Indian soil,
  Soon as the burning day was clos'd,
I could mock the sultry toil,
  When on my charmer's breast repos'd.
MACHEATH. And I would love you all the day,
POLLY. Every night would kiss and play,
MACHEATH. If with me you'd fondly stray
POLLY. Over the hills and far away.

POLLY. Yes, I would go with thee. But oh!—how shall I speak it? I must be torn from thee. We must part.

MACHEATH. How! Part!

POLLY. We must, we must.—My papa and mama are set against thy life. They now, even now are in search after thee. They are preparing evidence against thee. Thy life depends upon a moment.

AIR XVII. *Gin thou wert mine awn thing.*

O what pain it is to part!
Can I leave thee, can I leave thee?
O what pain it is to part!
Can thy Polly ever leave thee?
But lest death my love should thwart,
And bring thee to the fatal cart,
Thus I tear thee from my bleeding heart!
Fly hence, and let me leave thee.

One kiss and then—one kiss—begone—farewell.

MACHEATH. My hand, my heart, my dear, is so riveted to thine, that I cannot unloose my hold.

POLLY. But my papa may intercept thee, and then I should lose the very glimmering of hope. A few weeks, perhaps, may reconcile us all. Shall thy Polly hear from thee?

MACHEATH. Must I go then?

POLLY. And will not absence change your love?

MACHEATH. If you doubt it, let me stay—and be hang'd.

POLLY. O how I fear! how I tremble!—Go—but when safety will give you leave, you will be sure to see me again; for 'till then Polly is wretched.

AIR XVIII. *O the broom, etc.*

(Parting, and looking back at each other with fondness; he at one door, she at the other.)

MACHEATH. The miser thus a shilling sees,
    Which he's oblig'd to pay,
    With sighs resigns it by degrees,
    And fears 'tis gone for aye.
POLLY. The boy, thus, when his sparrow's flown,
    The bird in silence eyes;
    But soon as out of sight 'tis gone,
    Whines, whimpers, sobs and cries.

Act II

A tavern near Newgate

JEMMY TWITCHER, CROOK-FINGERED JACK, WAT
DREARY, ROBIN OF BAGSHOT, NIMMING NED, HENRY
PADINGTON, MATT OF THE MINT, BEN BUDGE, *and the
rest of the gang, at the table, with wine, brandy
and tobacco.*[1]

BEN. But pr'ythee, Matt, what is become of thy
brother Tom? I have not seen him since my return
from transportation.

MATT. Poor brother Tom had an accident this time
twelve-month, and so clever a made fellow he was,
that I could not save him from those fleaing[2] rascals
the surgeons; and now, poor man, he is among the
otamys[3] at Surgeon's Hall.

BEN. So it seems, his time was come.

JEM. But the present time is ours, and no body alive
hath more. Why are the laws levell'd at us? are we
more dishonest than the rest of mankind? What we
win, gentlemen, is our own by the law of arms, and
the right of conquest.

CROOK. Where shall we find such another set of
practical philosophers, who to a man are above the
fear of death?

WAT. Sound men, and true!

ROBIN. Of try'd courage, and indefatigable industry!

NED. Who is there here that would not dye for his
friend?

HARRY. Who is there here that would betray him for
his interest?

[1] The colorful nicknames which Gay gives the members of the
gang are only slight exaggerations of those common among the
criminals of the day. See, for instance, "Newgate's Garland"
(page 85.)   [2] **fleaing** from "flay," to skin or fleece   [3] **otamys**
anatomies, skeletons

MATT. Show me a gang of courtiers that can say as much.

BEN. We are for a just partition of the world, for every man hath a right to enjoy life.

MATT. We retrench the superfluities of mankind. The world is avaritious, and I hate avarice. A covetous fellow, like a jack-daw, steals what he was never made to enjoy, for the sake of hiding it. These are the robbers of mankind, for money was made for the free-hearted and generous, and where is the injury of taking from another, what he hath not the heart to make use of?

JEM. Our several stations for the day are fixt. Good luck attend us all. Fill the glasses.

AIR XIX. *Fill ev'ry glass, etc.*

MATT. Fill ev'ry glass, for wine inspires us,
And fires us
With courage, love and joy.
Women and wine should life employ.
Is there ought else on earth desirous?
CHORUS. Fill ev'ry glass, etc.

SCENE II

(To them enter MACHEATH*)*

MACHEATH. Gentlemen, well met. My heart hath been with you this hour; but an unexpected affair hath detain'd me. No ceremony, I beg you.

MATT. We were just breaking up to go upon duty. Am I to have the honour of taking the air with you, sir, this evening upon the Heath? I drink a dram now and then with the stage-coachmen in the way of friendship and intelligence; and I know that about this time there will be passengers upon the Western Road who are worth speaking with.

MACHEATH. I was to have been of that party—but—
MATT. But what, sir?

MACHEATH. Is there any man who suspects my courage?

MATT. We have all been witnesses of it.

MACHEATH. My honour and truth to the gang?

MATT. I'll be answerable for it.

MACHEATH. In the division of our booty, have I ever shown the least marks of avarice or injustice?

MATT. By these questions something seems to have ruffled you. Are any of us suspected?

MACHEATH. I have a fixt confidence, gentlemen, in you all, as men of honour, and as such I value and respect you. Peachum is a man that is useful to us.

MATT. Is he about to play us any foul play? I'll shoot him through the head.

MACHEATH. I beg you, gentlemen, act with conduct and discretion. A pistol is your last resort.

MATT. He knows nothing of this meeting.

MACHEATH. Business cannot go on without him. He is a man who knows the world, and is a necessary agent to us. We have had a slight difference, and till it is accommodated I shall be oblig'd to keep out of his way. Any private dispute of mine shall be of no ill consequence to my friends. You must continue to act under his direction, for the moment we break loose from him, our gang is ruin'd.[1]

MATT. As a bawd [2] to a whore, I grant you, he is to us of great convenience.

MACHEATH. Make him believe I have quitted the gang, which I can never do but with life. At our private quarters I will continue to meet you. A week or so will probably reconcile us.

MATT. Your instructions shall be observ'd. 'Tis now high time for us to repair to our several duties; so till the evening at our quarters in Moor-fields[3] we bid you farewell.

[1] a parable of the political situation in England: George II, like Macheath, is the nominal ruler but Walpole, like Peachum, controls the purse strings and is the real power   [2] bawd procurer
[3] Moor-fields recreation grounds near London, used by highwaymen as a meeting place

MACHEATH. I shall wish my self with you. Success
attend you.

(Sits down melancholy at the table)

AIR XX. *March in Rinaldo,*[4] *with drums and trumpets.*

MATT. Let us take the road.
　　Hark! I hear the sound of coaches!
　　The hour of attack approaches,
　　To your arms, brave boys, and load.
　　See the ball I hold!
　　Let the chymists[5] toil like asses,
　　Our fire their fire surpasses,
　　And turns all our lead to gold.

*(The gang, rang'd in the front of the stage, load their
pistols, and stick them under their girdles; then go off
singing the first part in chorus.)*

SCENE III

MACHEATH, DRAWER

MACHEATH. What a fool is a fond wench! Polly is
most confoundedly bit.—I love the sex. And a man
who loves money, might as well be contented with
one guinea, as I with one woman. The town perhaps
hath been as much oblig'd to me, for recruiting it
with free-hearted ladies, as to any recruiting officer in
the army.[1] If it were not for us and the other gentlemen of the sword, Drury-Lane would be uninhabited.

AIR XXI. *Would you have a young virgin, etc.*

If the heart of a man is deprest with cares,
The mist is dispell'd when a woman appears;
Like the notes of a fiddle, she sweetly, sweetly
Raises the spirits, and charms our ears.
Roses and lillies her cheeks disclose,

[4] **Rinaldo** an opera by Handel　[5] **chymists** alchemists. The gang
does a better job of turning lead to gold
[1] **recruiting officer . . . army** the recruiting officer enlists sol-
diers who, in turn, attract camp followers

> But her ripe lips are more sweet than those.
> Press her,
> Caress her,
> With blisses,
> Her kisses
> Dissolve us in pleasure, and soft repose.

I must have women. There is nothing unbends the mind like them. Money is not so strong a cordial for the time.—Drawer.—(*Enter Drawer*) Is the porter gone for all the ladies, according to my directions?

DRAWER. I expect him back every minute. But you know, sir, you sent him as far as Hockley in the Hole, for three of the ladies, for one in Vinegar Yard, and for the rest of them somewhere about Lewkner's Lane.[2] Sure some of them are below, for I hear the bar bell. As they come I will show them up.—Coming, coming.

SCENE IV

MACHEATH, MRS. COAXER, DOLLY TRULL, MRS. VIXEN, BETTY DOXY, JENNY DIVER, MRS. SLAMMEKIN, SUKY TAWDRY, *and* MOLLY BRAZEN

MACHEATH. Dear Mrs. Coaxer, you are welcome. You look charmingly to-day. I hope you don't want[1] the repairs of quality, and lay on paint—Dolly Trull! kiss me, you slut; are you as amorous as ever, hussy? You are always so taken up with stealing hearts, that you don't allow your self time to steal any thing else. —Ah Dolly, thou wilt ever be a coquette!—Mrs. Vixen, I'm yours, I always lov'd a woman of wit and spirit; they make charming mistresses, but plaguy wives.— Betty Doxy! Come hither, hussy. Do you drink as hard as ever? You had better stick to good wholesome beer; for in troth, Betty, strong-waters[2] will in time ruin your constitution. You should leave those to your

---

[2] **Hockley, Vinegar Yard, Lewkner's Lane** all disreputable districts
[1] **want** require [2] **strong-waters** hard liquor

betters.—What! and my pretty Jenny Diver too! As
prim and demure as ever! There is not any prude,
though ever so high bred, hath a more sanctify'd look,
with a more mischievous heart. Ah! thou art a dear artful hypocrite.—Mrs. Slammekin! as careless and genteel as ever! all you fine ladies, who know your own
beauty, affect an undress[3]—but see, here's Suky
Tawdry come to contradict what I was saying. Every
thing she gets one way she lays out upon her back.
Why, Suky, you must keep at least a dozen tally-men.[4]
Molly Brazen! (*She kisses him.*) That's well done. I
love a free-hearted wench. Thou hast a most agreeable
assurance, girl, and art as willing as a turtle.—But
hark! I hear musick. The harper is at the door. *If
musick be the food of love, play on.*[5] E'er you seat
your selves, ladies, what think you of a dance? Come
in. (*Enter harper*) Play the French tune, that Mrs.
Slammekin was so fond of.

(*A dance à la ronde in the French manner; near the
end of it this song and chorus*)

AIR XXII. *Cotillon.*

Youth's the season made for joys,
Love is then our duty;
She alone who that employs,
Well deserves her beauty.
Let's be gay,
While we may,
Beauty's a flower despis'd in decay.
Youth's the season, etc.

Let us drink and sport to-day,
Ours is not to-morrow.
Love with youth flies swift away,
Age is nought but sorrow.
Dance and sing,
Time's on the wing,

---

[3] **undress** informal dress   [4] **keep . . . tally-men** keep a dozen
installment merchants in business   [5] The first line of *Twelfth
Night*

Life never knows the return of spring.
CHORUS. Let us drink, etc.

MACHEATH. Now, pray ladies, take your places. Here, fellow. (*Pays the harper*) Bid the drawer bring us more wine. (*Exit harper*) If any of the ladies chuse gin, I hope they will be so free to call for it.

JENNY. You look as if you meant me. Wine is strong enough for me. Indeed, sir, I never drink strong-waters, but when I have the cholic.

MACHEATH. Just the excuse of the fine ladies! Why, a lady of quality is never without the cholic. I hope, Mrs. Coaxer, you have had good success of late in your visits among the mercers.[6]

COAXER. We have so many interlopers—Yet with industry, one may still have a little picking. I carried a silver-flower'd lutestring and a piece of black padesoy[7] to Mr. Peachum's lock but last week.

VIXEN. There's Molly Brazen hath the ogle of a rattlesnake. She rivitted a linnen-draper's eye so fast upon her, that he was nick'd of three pieces of cambric[8] before he could look off.

BRAZEN. O dear madam!—But sure nothing can come up to your handling of laces! And then you have such a sweet deluding tongue! To cheat a man is nothing; but the woman must have fine parts[9] indeed who cheats a woman!

VIXEN. Lace, madam lyes in a small compass, and is of easy conveyance. But you are apt, madam, to think too well of your friends.

COAXER. If any woman hath more art than another, to be sure, 'tis Jenny Diver. Though her fellow be never so agreeable, she can pick his pocket as cooly, as if money were her only pleasure. Now that is a command of the passions uncommon in a woman!

JENNY. I never go to the tavern with a man, but in

---

[6] mercers dry goods merchants [7] lutestring . . . padesoy expensive fabrics [8] nick'd . . . cambric "relieved of" three pieces of fine linen. Molly, Mrs. Vixen and Mrs. Coaxer are shoplifters [9] fine parts shrewdness

the view of business. I have other hours, and other sort of men for my pleasure. But had I your address, madam—

MACHEATH. Have done with your compliments, ladies; and drink about: You are not so fond of me, Jenny, as you use to be.

JENNY. 'Tis not convenient, sir, to show my fondness among so many rivals. 'Tis your own choice, and not the warmth of my inclination, that will determine you.

AIR XXIII. *All in a misty morning*.

Before the barn-door crowing,
The cock by hens attended,
His eyes around him throwing,
Stands for a while suspended.
Then one he singles from the crew,
And cheers the happy hen;
With how do you do, and how do you do,
And how do you do again.

MACHEATH. Ah Jenny! thou art a dear slut.

TRULL. Pray, madam, were you ever in keeping?

TAWDRY. I hope, madam, I han't been so long upon the town, but I have met with some good fortune as well as my neighbours.

TRULL. Pardon me, madam, I meant no harm by the question; 'twas only in the way of conversation.

TAWDRY. Indeed, madam, if I had not been a fool, I might have liv'd very handsomely with my last friend. But upon his missing five guineas, he turn'd me off. Now I never suspected he had counted them.

SLAMMEKIN. Who do you look upon, madam, as your best sort of keepers?

TRULL. That, madam, is thereafter as they be.

SLAMMEKIN. I, madam, was once kept by a Jew; and bating[10] their religion, to women they are a good sort of people.

[10] **bating** excluding

TAWDRY. Now for my part, I own I like an old fellow: for we always make them pay for what they can't do.

VIXEN. A spruce prentice, let me tell you, ladies, is no ill thing, they bleed freely. I have sent at least two or three dozen of them in my time to the plantations.[11]

JENNY. But to be sure, sir, with so much good fortune as you have had upon the road, you must be grown immensely rich.

MACHEATH. The road, indeed, hath done me justice, but the gaming-table hath been my ruin.

AIR XXIV. *When once I lay with another man's wife.*

> JENNY. The gamesters and lawyers are jugglers alike,
>   If they meddle your all is in danger:
>   Like gypsies, if once they can finger a souse,[12]
>   Your pockets they pick, and they pilfer your house,
>   And give your estate to a stranger.

A man of courage should never put any thing to the risque, but his life. These are the tools of a man of honour. Cards and dice are only fit for cowardly cheats, who prey upon their friends.

(*She takes up his pistol.* TAWDRY *takes up the other.*)

TAWDRY. This, sir, is fitter for your hand. Besides your loss of money, 'tis a loss to the ladies. Gaming takes you off from women. How fond could I be of you! but before company, 'tis ill bred.

MACHEATH. Wanton hussies!

JENNY. I must and will have a kiss to give my wine a zest.

(*They take him about the neck, and make signs to* PEACHUM *and Constables, who rush in upon him.*)

---

[11] **A spruce prentice . . . plantations** an apprentice lavishly spends money stolen from his master and when caught, is transported   [12] **souse** sou

Scene V

(*To them* Peachum *and Constables*)

Peachum. I seize you, sir, as my prisoner.

Macheath. Was this well done, Jenny?—Women are decoy ducks; who can trust them! Beasts, jades, jilts, harpies, furies, whores!

Peachum. Your case, Mr. Macheath, is not particular. The greatest heroes have been ruin'd by women. But, to do them justice, I must own they are a pretty sort of creatures, if we could trust them. You must now, sir, take your leave of the ladies, and if they have a mind to make you a visit, they will be sure to find you at home. The gentleman, ladies, lodges in Newgate. Constables, wait upon the captain to his lodgings.

Air XXV. *When first I laid siege to my Chloris.*

Macheath. At the tree I shall suffer with pleasure,
At the tree I shall suffer with pleasure,
Let me go where I will,
In all kinds of ill,
I shall find no such furies as these are.

Peachum. Ladies, I'll take care the reckoning shall be discharg'd.

(*Exeunt* Macheath, *guarded with* Peachum *and Constables*)

Scene VI

(*The women remain*)

Vixen. Look ye, Mrs. Jenny, though Mr. Peachum may have made a private bargain with you and Suky Tawdry for betraying the captain, as we were all assisting, we ought all to share alike.

Coaxer. I think Mr. Peachum, after so long an acquaintance, might have trusted me as well as Jenny Diver.

SLAMMEKIN. I am sure at least three men of his hanging, and in a year's time too, (if he did me justice) should be set down to my account.

TRULL. Mrs. Slammekin, that is not fair. For you know one of them was taken in bed with me.

JENNY. As far as a bowl of punch or a treat, I believe Mrs. Suky will join with me.—As for any thing else, ladies, you cannot in conscience expect it.

SLAMMEKIN. Dear madam—

TRULL. I would not for the world—

SLAMMEKIN. 'Tis impossible for me—

TRULL. As I hope to be sav'd, madam—

SLAMMEKIN. Nay, then I must stay here all night—

TRULL. Since you command me.

(*Exeunt with great ceremony*)

SCENE VII

Newgate

LOCKIT, *Turnkeys*, MACHEATH, *Constables*

LOCKIT. Noble captain, you are welcome. You have not been a lodger of mine this year and half. You know the custom, sir. Garnish,[1] captain, garnish. Hand me down those fetters there.

MACHEATH. Those, Mr. Lockit, seem to be the heaviest of the whole set. With your leave, I should like the further pair better.

LOCKIT. Look ye, captain, we know what is fittest for our prisoners. When a gentleman uses me with civility, I always do the best I can to please him— Hand them down I say—We have them of all prices, from one guinea to ten, and 'tis fitting every gentleman should please himself.

MACHEATH. I understand you, sir. (*Gives money*) The fees here are so many, and so exorbitant, that few fortunes can bear the expence of getting off handsomly, or of dying like a gentleman.

[1] **Garnish** a bribe to insure better treatment

LOCKIT. Those, I see, will fit the captain better.—
Take down the further pair. Do but examine them,
sir—never was better work.—How genteely they are
made!—They will fit as easy as a glove, and the nicest
man in England might not be asham'd to wear them.
(*He puts on the chains.*) If I had the best gentleman
in the land in my custody I could not equip him more
handsomly. And so, sir—I now leave you to your
private meditations.

Scene VIII

Macheath

AIR XXVI. *Courtiers, courtiers think it no harm.*

> Man may escape from rope and gun;
> Nay, some have out-liv'd the doctor's pill:
> Who takes a woman must be undone,
> That basilisk[1] is sure to kill.
> The fly that sips treacle is lost in the sweets,
> So he that tastes woman, woman, woman,
> He that tastes woman, ruin meets.

To what a woful plight have I brought my self! Here
must I (all day long, 'till I am hang'd) be confin'd
to hear the reproaches of a wench who lays her ruin
at my door.—I am in the custody of her father, and to
be sure if he knows of the matter, I shall have a fine
time on't betwixt this and my execution.—But I
promis'd the wench marriage.—What signifies a promise to a woman? does not man in marriage itself
promise a hundred things that he never means to perform? Do all we can, women will believe us; for they
look upon a promise as an excuse for following their
own inclinations.—But here comes Lucy, and I cannot
get from her—wou'd I were deaf!

[1] basilisk a mythical serpent whose very look was deadly

Scene IX

Macheath, Lucy

Lucy. You base man, you,—how can you look me in the face after what hath past between us?—See here, perfidious wretch, how I am forc'd to bear about the load of infamy you have laid upon me—O Macheath! thou hast robb'd me of my quiet—to see thee tortur'd would give me pleasure.

Air XXVII. *A lovely lass to a friar came.*

Thus when a good huswife sees a rat
In her trap in the morning taken,
With pleasure her heart goes pit a pat,
In revenge for her loss of bacon.
Then she throws him
To the dog or cat,
To be worried, crush'd and shaken.

Macheath. Have you no bowels, no tenderness, my dear Lucy, to see a husband in these circumstances?

Lucy. A husband!

Macheath. In ev'ry respect but the form, and that, my dear, may be said over us at any time.—Friends should not insist upon ceremonies. From a man of honour, his word is as good as his bond.

Lucy. 'Tis the pleasure of all you fine men to insult the women you have ruin'd.

Air XXVIII. *'Twas when the sea was roaring.*[1]

How cruel are the traytors,
Who lye and swear in jest,
To cheat unguarded creatures

[1] an instance of Gay's borrowing from himself. This ballad, with music attributed to Handel, first appeared in Gay's play, *The What D'ye Call It* (1715), and had become a popular favorite. So, too, the music for Air XXXIV ("Thus when the swallow, seeking prey") was originally written for Gay's ballad, *Sweet William's Farewell to Black-Ey'd Susan* (1720)

Of virtue, fame, and rest!
Whoever steals a shilling,
Thro' shame the guilt conceals:
In love the perjur'd villain
With boasts the theft reveals.

MACHEATH. The very first opportunity, my dear,
(have but patience) you shall be my wife in whatever
manner you please.

LUCY. Insinuating monster! And so you think I know
nothing of the affair of Miss Polly Peachum.—I could
tear thy eyes out!

MACHEATH. Sure Lucy, you can't be such a fool as
to be jealous of Polly!

LUCY. Are you not married to her, you brute, you?

MACHEATH. Married! Very good. The wench gives
it out only to vex thee, and to ruin me in thy good
opinion. 'Tis true, I go to the house; I chat with the
girl, I kiss her, I say a thousand things to her (as all
gentlemen do) that mean nothing, to divert my self;
and now the silly jade hath set it about that I am
married to her, to let me know what she would be at.
Indeed, my dear Lucy, these violent passions may be
of ill consequence to a woman in your condition.

LUCY. Come, come, captain, for all your assurance,
you know that Miss Polly hath put it out of your
power to do me the justice you promis'd me.

MACHEATH. A jealous woman believes ev'ry thing
her passion suggests. To convince you of my sincerity,
if we can find the ordinary, I shall have no scruples
of making you my wife; and I know the consequence
of having two at a time.

LUCY. That you are only to be hang'd, and so get
rid of them both.

MACHEATH. I am ready, my dear Lucy, to give you
satisfaction—if you think there is any in marriage.—
What can a man of honour say more?

LUCY. So then it seems, you are not married to
Miss Polly?

MACHEATH. You know, Lucy, the girl is prodigiously

conceited. No man can say a civil thing to her, but (like other fine ladies) her vanity makes her think he's her own for ever and ever.

AIR XXIX. *The sun had loos'd his weary teams.*

> The first time at the looking-glass
> The mother sets her daughter,
> The image strikes the smiling lass
> With self-love ever after.
> Each time she looks, she, fonder grown,
> Thinks ev'ry charm grows stronger:
> But alas, vain maid, all eyes but your own
> Can see you are not younger.

When women consider their own beauties, they are all alike unreasonable in their demands; for they expect their lovers should like them as long as they like themselves.

LUCY. Yonder is my father—perhaps this way we may light upon the ordinary, who shall try if you will be as good as your word.—For I long to be made an honest woman.

SCENE X

PEACHUM, LOCKIT *with an account-book*

LOCKIT. In this last affair, brother Peachum, we are agreed. You have consented to go halves in Macheath.

PEACHUM. We shall never fall out about an execution.—But as to that article, pray how stands our last year's account?

LOCKIT. If you will run your eye over it, you'll find 'tis fair and clearly stated.

PEACHUM. This long arrear of the government is very hard upon us![1] Can it be expected that we should hang our acquaintance for nothing, when our betters will hardly save theirs without being paid for it. Un-

---

[1] The government is in arrears on payments of rewards for criminals whom Peachum and Lockit have betrayed

less the people in employment[2] pay better, I promise
them for the future, I shall let other rogues live besides their own.

LOCKIT. Perhaps, brother, they are afraid these
matters may be carried too far. We are treated too by
them with contempt, as if our profession were not
reputable.

PEACHUM. In one respect indeed, our employment
may be reckon'd dishonest, because, like great statesmen, we encourage those who betray their friends.

LOCKIT. Such language, brother, any where else,
might turn to your prejudice. Learn to be more
guarded, I beg you.

AIR XXX. *How happy are we, etc.*

> When you censure the age,
> Be cautious and sage,
> Lest the courtiers offended should be:
> If you mention vice or bribe,
> 'Tis so pat to all the tribe;
> Each cries—That was levell'd at me.

PEACHUM. Here's poor Ned Clincher's name, I see.
Sure, brother Lockit, there was a little unfair proceed-
ing in Ned's case: for he told me in the condemn'd
hold, that for value receiv'd, you had promis'd him a
Session or two longer without molestation.

LOCKIT. Mr. Peachum,—this is the first time my
honour was ever call'd in question.

PEACHUM. Business is at an end—if once we act
dishonourably.

LOCKIT. Who accuses me?

PEACHUM. You are warm, brother.

LOCKIT. He that attacks my honour, attacks my
livelyhood.—And this usage—sir—is not to be born.

PEACHUM. Since you provoke me to speak—I must
tell you too, that Mrs. Coaxer charges you with de-
frauding her of her information-money, for the ap-

---

[2] **people in employment** government officials

prehending of curl-pated Hugh. Indeed, indeed, brother, we must punctually pay our spies, or we shall have no information.

LOCKIT. Is this language to me, sirrah—who have sav'd you from the gallows, sirrah! (*Collaring each other*)

PEACHUM. If I am hang'd, it shall be for ridding the world of an arrant rascal.

LOCKIT. This hand shall do the office of the halter[8] you deserve, and throttle you—you dog!

PEACHUM. Brother, brother,—we are both in the wrong—we shall be both losers in the dispute—for you know we have it in our power to hang each other. You should not be so passionate.

LOCKIT. Nor you so provoking.

PEACHUM. 'Tis our mutual interest; 'tis for the interest of the world we should agree. If I said any thing, brother, to the prejudice of your character, I ask pardon.

LOCKIT. Brother Peachum—I can forgive as well as resent.—Give me your hand. Suspicion does not become a friend.

PEACHUM. I only meant to give you occasion to justifie yourself: But I must now step home, for I expect the gentleman about this snuff-box, that Filch nimm'd two nights ago in the park. I appointed him at this hour.

SCENE XI

LOCKIT, LUCY

LOCKIT. Whence come you, hussy?

LUCY. My tears might answer that question.

LOCKIT. You have then been whimpering and fondling, like a spaniel, over the fellow that hath abus'd you.

LUCY. One can't help love; one can't cure it. 'Tis not in my power to obey you, and hate him.

[8] halter hangman's rope

LOCKIT. Learn to bear your husband's death like a reasonable woman. 'Tis not the fashion, now-a-days, so much as to affect sorrow upon these occasions. No woman would every marry, if she had not the chance of mortality for a release. Act like a woman of spirit, hussy, and thank your father for what he is doing.

AIR XXXI. *Of a noble race was Shenkin.*

LUCY. Is then his fate decreed, sir?
　　Such a man can I think of quitting?
　　When first we met, so moves me yet,
　　O see how my heart is splitting!

LOCKIT. Look ye, Lucy—there is no saving him.—So, I think, you must ev'n do like other widows—buy your self weeds, and be cheerful.

AIR XXXII.

You'll think, e'er many days ensue,
This sentence not severe;
I hang your husband, child, 'tis true,
But with him hang your care.
Twang dang dillo dee.

Like a good wife, go moan over your dying husband. That, child, is your duty—consider, girl, you can't have the man and the money too—so make yourself as easy as you can by getting all you can from him.

SCENE XII

LUCY, MACHEATH

LUCY. Though the ordinary was out of the way to-day, I hope, my dear, you will, upon the first opportunity, quiet my scruples—Oh sir!—my father's hard heart is not to be soften'd, and I am in the utmost despair.

MACHEATH. But if I could raise a small sum—would not twenty guineas, think you, move him?—Of all the arguments in the way of business, the perquisite is the most prevailing.—Your father's perquisites for the escape of prisoners must amount to a considerable sum in the year. Money well tim'd, and properly apply'd, will do any thing.

AIR XXXIII. *London ladies.*

If you at an office solicit your due,
And would not have matters neglected;
You must quicken the clerk with the perquisite too,
To do what his duty directed.
Or would you the frowns of a lady prevent,
She too has this palpable failing,
The perquisite softens her into consent;
That reason with all is prevailing.

LUCY. What love or money can do shall be done: for all my comfort depends upon your safety.

SCENE XIII

LUCY, MACHEATH, POLLY

POLLY. Where is my dear husband?—Was a rope ever intended for this neck!—O let me throw my arms about it, and throttle thee with love!—Why dost thou turn away from me?—'Tis thy Polly—'tis thy wife.

MACHEATH. Was ever such an unfortunate rascal as I am!

LUCY. Was there ever such another villain!

POLLY. O Macheath! was it for this we parted? Taken! Imprison'd! Try'd! Hang'd!—cruel reflection! I'll stay with thee 'till death—no force shall tear thy dear wife from thee now.—What means my love?— Not one kind word! not one kind look! think what thy Polly suffers to see thee in this condition.

AIR XXXIV. *All in the Downs, etc.*

Thus when the swallow, seeking prey,
Within the sash is closely pent,
His consort with bemoaning lay,
Without sits pining for th' event.
Her chatt'ring lovers all around her skim;
She heeds them not (poor bird) her soul's with him.

MACHEATH. I must disown her. (*Aside*) The wench is distracted.

LUCY. Am I then bilk'd of my virtue? Can I have no reparation? Sure men were born to lye, and women to believe them! O villain! Villain!

POLLY. Am I not thy wife?—Thy neglect of me, thy aversion to me too severely proves it.—Look on me. —Tell me, am I not thy wife?

LUCY. Perfidious wretch!

POLLY. Barbarous husband!

LUCY. Hadst thou been hang'd five months ago, I had been happy.

POLLY. And I too—If you had been kind to me 'till death, it would not have vex'd me—And that's no very unreasonable request, (though from a wife) to a man who hath not above seven or eight days to live.

LUCY. Art thou then married to another? Hast thou two wives, monster?

MACHEATH. If women's tongues can cease for an answer—hear me.

LUCY. I won't.—Flesh and blood can't bear my usage.

POLLY. Shall I not claim my own? Justice bids me speak.

AIR XXXV. *Have you heard of a frolicksome ditty.*

MACHEATH. How happy could I be with either,
　　Were t'other dear charmer away!
　　But while you thus teaze me together,
　　To neither a word will I say;
　　But tol de rol, etc.

POLLY. Sure, my dear, there ought to be some preference shown to a wife! At least she may claim the appearance of it. He must be distracted with his misfortunes, or he cou'd not use me thus!

LUCY. O villain, villain! thou hast deceiv'd me—I could even inform against thee with pleasure. Not a prude wishes more heartily to have facts against her **intim**ate acquaintance, than I now wish to have facts against thee. I would have her satisfaction, and they should all out.

AIR XXXVI. Irish trot.

POLLY. I'm bubbled.
LUCY. —I'm bubbled.
POLLY. Oh how I am troubled!
LUCY. Bambouzled, and bit! [1]
POLLY. —My distresses are doubled.
LUCY. When you come to the tree, should the hangman refuse, These fingers, with pleasure, could fasten the noose.
POLLY. I'm bubbled, etc.

MACHEATH. Be pacified, my dear Lucy—This is all a fetch[2] of Polly's to make me desperate with you in case I get off. If I am hang'd, she would fain have the credit of being thought my widow—Really, Polly, this is no time for a dispute of this sort; for whenever you are talking of marriage, I am thinking of hanging.

POLLY. And hast thou the heart to persist in disowning me?

MACHEATH. And hast thou the heart to persist in persuading me that I am married? Why, Polly, dost thou seek to aggravate my misfortunes?

LUCY. Really, Miss Peachum, you but expose yourself. Besides, 'tis barbarous in you to worry a gentleman in his circumstances.

AIR XXXVII.

POLLY. Cease your funning;
   Force or cunning
   Never shall my heart trapan.[3]
   All these sallies
   Are but malice
   To seduce my constant man.
   'Tis most certain,
   By their flirting
   Women oft have envy shown:

[1] bubbled . . . bit cheated   [2] fetch trick   [3] trapan trepan, deceive

Pleas'd, to ruin
Others wooing;
Never happy in their own!

POLLY. Decency, madam, methinks might teach you
to behave yourself with some reserve with the husband, while his wife is present.

MACHEATH. But seriously, Polly, this is carrying the
joke a little too far.

LUCY. If you are determin'd, madam, to raise a dis-
turbance in the prison, I shall be oblig'd to send for
the turnkey to shew you the door. I am sorry, madam,
you force me to be so ill-bred.

POLLY. Give me leave to tell you, madam; these
forward airs don't become you in the least, madam.
And my duty, madam, obliges me to stay with my
husband, madam.

AIR XXXVIII. *Good-morrow, gossip Joan.*

LUCY. Why how now, madam flirt?
    If you thus must chatter,
    And are for slinging dirt,
    Let's try who best can spatter;

                    madam flirt!

POLLY. Why how now, saucy jade;
    Sure the wench is tipsy!
    How can you see me made   (*To him*)
    The scoff of such a gipsy?
                    saucy jade!   (*To her*)

SCENE XIV

LUCY, MACHEATH, POLLY, PEACHUM

PEACHUM. Where's my wench? Ah hussy! hussy!—
Come you home, you slut; and when your fellow is
hang'd, hang yourself, to make your family some
amends.

POLLY. Dear, dear father, do not tear me from him—
I must speak; I have more to say to him—Oh! twist

thy fetters about me, that he may not haul me from thee!

PEACHUM. Sure all women are alike! If ever they commit the folly, they are sure to commit another by exposing themselves—Away—Not a word more—You are my prisoner now, hussy.

AIR XXXIX. *Irish howl.*

POLLY. No power on earth can e'er divide
The knot that sacred love hath ty'd.
When parents draw against our mind,
The true-love's knot they faster bind.
Oh, oh ray, oh amborah—oh, oh, etc.

(*Holding* MACHEATH, PEACHUM *pulling her*)

SCENE XV

LUCY, MACHEATH

MACHEATH. I am naturally compassionate, wife; so that I could not use the wench as she deserv'd; which made you at first suspect there was something in what she said.

LUCY. Indeed, my dear, I was strangely puzzled.

MACHEATH. If that had been the case, her father would never have brought me into this circumstance —No, Lucy,—I had rather dye than be false to thee.

LUCY. How happy am I, if you say this from your heart! For I love thee so, that I could sooner bear to see thee hang'd than in the arms of another.

MACHEATH. But couldst thou bear to see me hang'd?

LUCY. O Macheath, I can never live to see that day.

MACHEATH. You see, Lucy, in the account of love you are in my debt; and you must now be convinc'd, that I rather chuse to die than be another's.—Make me, if possible, love thee more, and let me owe my life to thee—If you refuse to assist me, Peachum and your father will immediately put me beyond all means of escape.

LUCY. My father, I know, hath been drinking hard

with the prisoners: and I fancy he is now taking his nap in his own room—If I can procure the keys, shall I go off with thee, my dear?

MACHEATH. If we are together, 'twill be impossible to lye conceal'd. As soon as the search begins to be a little cool, I will send to thee—'Till then my heart is thy prisoner.

LUCY. Come then, my dear husband—owe thy life to me—and though you love me not—be grateful— But that Polly runs in my head strangely.

MACHEATH. A moment of time may make us unhappy for-ever.

AIR XL. *The lass of Patie's mill.*

LUCY. I like the fox shall grieve,
  Whose mate hath left her side,
  Whom hounds, from morn to eve,
  Chase o'er the country wide.
  Where can my lover hide?
  Where cheat the wary pack?
  If love be not his guide,
  He never will come back!

Act III

SCENE I

Newgate

LOCKIT, LUCY

LOCKIT. To be sure, wench, you must have been aiding and abetting to help him to this escape.

LUCY. Sir, here hath been Peachum and his daughter, Polly, and to be sure they know the ways of Newgate as well as if they had been born and bred in the place all their lives. Why must all your suspicion light upon me?

LOCKIT. Lucy, Lucy, I will have none of these shuffling answers.

LUCY. Well then—If I know any thing of him I wish I may be burnt!

LOCKIT. Keep your temper, Lucy, or I shall pronounce you guilty.

LUCY. Keep yours, sir,—I do wish I may be burnt. I do—And what can I say more to convince you?

LOCKIT. Did he tip handsomely?—How much did he come down with? Come hussy, don't cheat your father; and I shall not be angry with you—Perhaps, you have made a better bargain with him than I could have done—How much, my good girl?

LUCY. You know, sir, I am fond of him, and would have given money to have kept him with me.

LOCKIT. Ah Lucy! thy education might have put thee more upon thy guard; for a girl in the bar of an alehouse is always besieg'd.

LUCY. Dear sir, mention not my education—for 'twas to that I owe my ruin.

AIR XLI. *If love's a sweet passion, etc.*

When young at the bar you first taught me to score,[1]
And bid me be free of my lips, and no more;
I was kiss'd by the parson, the squire, and the sot:
When the guest was departed, the kiss was forgot.
But his kiss was so sweet, and so closely he prest,
That I languish'd and pin'd 'till I granted the rest.

If you can forgive me, sir, I will make a fair confession, for to be sure he hath been a most barbarous villain to me.

LOCKIT. And so you have let him escape, hussy—have you?

LUCY. When a woman loves; a kind look, a tender word can persuade her to any thing—and I could ask no other bribe.

LOCKIT. Thou wilt always be a vulgar slut, Lucy—If you would not be look'd upon as a fool, you should

[1] **score** keep count of drinks served

never do any thing but upon the foot of interest.
Those that act otherwise are their own bubbles.[2]

Lucy. But love, sir, is a misfortune that may happen
to the most discreet woman, and in love we are all
fools alike.—Notwithstanding all he swore, I am now
fully convinc'd that Polly Peachum is actually his
wife.—Did I let him escape, (fool that I was!) to go
to her?—Polly will wheedle her self into his money,
and then Peachum will hang him, and cheat us both.

Lockit. So I am to be ruin'd, because, forsooth, you
must be in love!—a very pretty excuse!

Lucy. I could murder that impudent happy strumpet:—I gave him his life, and that creature enjoys
the sweets of it.—Ungrateful Macheath!

AIR XLII. *South-sea Ballad.*

My love is all madness and folly,
Alone I lye,
Toss, tumble, and cry,
What a happy creature is Polly!
Was e'er such a wretch as I!
With rage I redden like scarlet,
That my dear inconstant varlet,
Stark blind to my charms,
Is lost in the arms
Of that jilt, that inveigling harlot!
Stark blind to my charms,
Is lost in the arms
Of that jilt, that inveigling harlot!
This, this my resentment alarms.

Lockit. And so, after all this mischief, I must stay
here to be entertain'd with your catterwauling, mistress Puss!—Out of my sight, wanton strumpet! you
shall fast and mortify yourself into reason, with now
and then a little handsome discipline to bring you to
your senses.—Go.

[2] **bubbles** dupes

Scene II

Lockit

Peachum then intends to outwit me in this affair; but I'll be even with him.—The dog is leaky in his liquor, so I'll ply him that way, get the secret from him, and turn this affair to my own advantage.—Lions, wolves, and vulturs don't live together in herds, droves or flocks.—Of all animals of prey, man is the only sociable one. Every one of us preys upon his neighbour, and yet we herd together.—Peachum is my companion, my friend—According to the custom of the world, indeed, he may quote thousands of precedents for cheating me—And shall not I make use of the privilege of friendship to make him a return?

AIR XLIII. *Packington's Pound.*

Thus gamesters united in friendship are found,
Though they know that their industry all is a cheat;
They flock to their prey at the dice-box's sound,
And join to promote one another's deceit.
But if by mishap
They fail of a chap,[1]
To keep in their hands, they each other entrap.
Like pikes, lank with hunger, who miss of their ends,
They bite their companions, and prey on their friends.

Now, Peachum, you and I, like honest tradesmen, are to have a fair tryal which of us two can over-reach the other.—Lucy.—(*Enter Lucy*) Are there any of Peachum's people now in the house?

Lucy. Filch, sir, is drinking a quartern of strong-waters in the next room with Black Moll.

Lockit. Bid him come to me.

---

[1] **fail . . . chap** lack a victim

Scene III

Lockit, Filch

Lockit. Why, boy, thou lookest as if thou wert half starv'd; like a shotten herring.[1]

Filch. One had need have the constitution of a horse to go through the business.—Since the favourite child-getter was disabled by a mis-hap, I have pick'd up a little money by helping the ladies to a pregnancy against their being call'd down to sentence.—But if a man cannot get an honest livelihood any easier way, I am sure, 'tis what I can't undertake for another Session.

Lockit. Truly, if that great man should tip off,[2] 'twould be an irreparable loss. The vigor and prowess of a knight-errant never sav'd half the ladies in distress that he hath done.—But, boy, can'st thou tell me where thy master is to be found?

Filch. At his lock, sir, at the Crooked Billet.

Lockit. Very well.—I have nothing more with you. (*Ex.* Filch) I'll go to him there, for I have many important affairs to settle with him; and in the way of those transactions, I'll artfully get into his secret.—So that Macheath shall not remain a day longer out of my clutches.

Scene IV

A gaming-house

(Macheath *in a fine tarnish'd coat*, Ben Budge, Matt of the Mint.)

Macheath. I am sorry, gentlemen, the road was so barren of money. When my friends are in difficulties, I am always glad that my fortune can be serviceable to them. (*Gives them money*) You see, gentlemen, I

---

[1] shotten herring after ejecting its spawn, the herring is lean and looks emaciated. See *I Henry IV*, II, iv, 143   [2] tip off die

am not a mere court friend, who professes every thing and will do nothing.

AIR XLIV. *Lillibulero.*

> The modes of the court so common are grown,
> That a true friend can hardly be met;
> Friendship for interest is but a loan,
> Which they let out for what they can get.
> 'Tis true, you find
> Some friends so kind,
> Who will give you good counsel themselves to defend.
> In sorrowful ditty,
> They promise, they pity,
> But shift you for money, from friend to friend.

But we, gentlemen, have still honour enough to break through the corruptions of the world.—And while I can serve you, you may command me.

BEN. It grieves my heart that so generous a man should be involv'd in such difficulties, as oblige him to live with such ill company, and herd with game-sters.

MATT. See the partiality of mankind!—One man may steal a horse, better than another look over a hedge.[1] —Of all mechanics, of all servile handycrafts-men, a gamester is the vilest. But yet, as many of the quality are of the profession, he is admitted amongst the politest company. I wonder we are not more respected.

MACHEATH. There will be deep play to-night at Marybone, and consequently money may be pick'd up upon the road. Meet me there, and I'll give you the hint who is worth setting.[2]

MATT. The fellow with a brown coat with a narrow gold binding, I am told, is never without money.

MACHEATH. What do you mean, Matt?—Sure you will not think of meddling with him!—He's a good honest kind of fellow, and one of us.

---

[1] One man . . . hedge roughly, one man's theft is condoned while the other is condemned for even thinking about it   [2] setting setting upon

BEN. To be sure, sir, we will put our selves under your direction.

MACHEATH. Have an eye upon the money-lenders. —A rouleau,[3] or two, would prove a pretty sort of an expedition. I hate extortion.

MATT. Those rouleaus are very pretty things.—I hate your bank bills—there is such a hazard in putting them off.

MACHEATH. There is a certain man of distinction, who in his time hath nick'd me out of a great deal of the ready. He is in my cash, Ben;—I'll point him out to you this evening, and you shall draw upon him for the debt.—The company are met. I hear the dice-box in the other room. So, gentlemen, your servant. You'll meet me at Marybone.

SCENE V

PEACHUM'S *lock.*

(*A table with wine, brandy, pipes and tobacco*)

PEACHUM, LOCKIT

LOCKIT. The Coronation account,[1] brother Peachum, is of so intricate a nature, that I believe it will never be settled.

PEACHUM. It consists indeed of a great variety of articles.—It was worth to our people, in fees of different kinds, above ten installments.—This is part of the account, brother, that lies open before us.

LOCKIT. A lady's tail of rich brocade—that, I see, is dispos'd of.

PEACHUM. To Mrs. Diana Trapes, the tally-woman,[2] and she will make a good hand on't in shoes and slippers, to trick out young ladies, upon their going into keeping.

LOCKIT. But I don't see any article of the jewels.

[3] rouleau roll of coins
[1] **Coronation account** covering disposal of items stolen from the crowd at George II's Coronation in 1727   [2] **tally-woman** see p. 32, n. 4

PEACHUM. Those are so well known, that they must be sent abroad—you'll find them enter'd under the article of exportation.—As for the snuff-boxes, watches, swords, etc.—I thought it best to enter them under their several heads.

LOCKIT. Seven and twenty women's pockets[3] compleat; with the several things therein contain'd; all seal'd, number'd, and enter'd.

PEACHUM. But, brother, it is impossible for us now to enter upon this affair.—We should have the whole day before us.—Besides, the account of the last half year's plate is in a book by it self, which lies at the other office.

LOCKIT. Bring us then more liquor.—To-day shall be for pleasure—to-morrow for business.—Ah brother, those daughters of ours are two slippery hussies—keep a watchful eye upon Polly, and Macheath in a day or two shall be our own again.

AIR XLV. *Down in the North Country.*

LOCKIT. What gudgeons[4] are we men!
    Ev'ry woman's easy prey.
    Though we have felt the hook, again
    We bite, and they betray.

    The bird that hath been trapt,
    When he hears his calling mate,
    To her he flies, again he's clapt
    Within the wiry grate.

PEACHUM. But what signifies catching the bird, if your daughter Lucy will set open the door of the cage?

LOCKIT. If men were answerable for the follies and frailties of their wives and daughters, no friends could keep a good correspondence together for two days.— This is unkind of you, brother; for among good friends, what they say or do goes for nothing.

(*Enter a servant*)

[3] **pockets** purses   [4] **gudgeons** small fish, easily caught

SERVANT. Sir, here's Mrs. Diana Trapes wants to speak with you.

PEACHUM. Shall we admit her, brother Lockit?

LOCKIT. By all means—she's a good customer, and a fine-spoken woman—and a woman who drinks and talks so freely will enliven the conversation.

PEACHUM. Desire her to walk in.

(*Exit servant*)

SCENE VI

PEACHUM, LOCKIT, MRS. TRAPES

PEACHUM. Dear Mrs. Dye, your servant—one may know by your kiss, that your ginn is excellent.

TRAPES. I was always very curious[1] in my liquors.

LOCKIT. There is no perfum'd breath like it—I have been long acquainted with the flavour of those lips—han't I, Mrs. Dye?

TRAPES. Fill it up.—I take as large draughts of liquor, as I did of love.—I hate a flincher in either.

AIR XLVI. *A Shepherd kept sheep, etc.*

In the days of my youth I could bill like a dove, fa, la, la, etc.
Like a sparrow at all times was ready for love, fa, la, la, etc.
The life of all mortals in kissing should pass,
Lip to lip while we're young—then the lip to the glass, fa, la, etc.

But now, Mr. Peachum, to our business.—If you have blacks of any kind, brought in of late; mantoes[2]—velvet scarfs—petticoats—let it be what it will—I am your chap—for all my ladies are very fond of mourning.

PEACHUM. Why, look ye, Mrs. Dye—you deal so

[1] **curious** particular   [2] **mantoes** manteaus, a loose robe or mantle

hard with us, that we can afford to give the gentlemen, who venture their lives for the goods, little or nothing.

TRAPES. The hard times oblige me to go very near in my dealing.—To be sure, of late years I have been a great sufferer by the parliament.—Three thousand pounds would hardly make me amends.—The Act for destroying the Mint[3] was a severe cut upon our business—'till then, if a customer stept out of the way—we knew where to have her—no doubt you know Mrs. Coaxer—there's a wench now ('till to-day) with a good suit of cloaths of mine upon her back, and I could never set eyes upon her for three months together.—Since the Act too against imprisonment for small sums, my loss there too hath been very considerable, and it must be so, when a lady can borrow a handsome petticoat, or a clean gown, and I not have the least hank[4] upon her! And, o' my conscience, now-a-days most ladies take a delight in cheating, when they can do it with safety.

PEACHUM. Madam, you had a handsome gold watch of us t'other day for seven guineas.—Considering we must have our profit—to a gentleman upon the road, a gold watch will be scarce worth the taking.

TRAPES. Consider, Mr. Peachum, that watch was remarkable,[5] and not of very safe sale.—If you have any black velvet scarfs—they are a handsome winter wear; and take with most gentlemen who deal with my customers.—'Tis I that put the ladies upon a good foot. 'Tis not youth or beauty that fixes their price. The gentlemen always pay according to their dress, from half a crown to two guineas; and yet those hussies make nothing of bilking of me.—Then too,

---

[3] **The Act . . . Mint** the Mint was an area in Southwark which served as a sanctuary for insolvent debtors and wanted criminals. (See also *Moll Flanders*). In 1724 an Act was passed cleaning up the area and enforcing the law   [4] **hank** hold   [5] **remarkable** distinctive, thus easily identified

allowing for accidents.—I have eleven fine customers now down under the surgeon's hands,[6]—what with fees and other expences, there are great goings-out, and no comings-in, and not a farthing to pay for at least a month's cloathing.—We run great risques— great risques indeed.

PEACHUM. As I remember, you said something just now of Mrs. Coaxer.

TRAPES. Yes, sir.—To be sure I stript her of a suit of my own cloaths about two hours ago; and have left her as she should be, in her shift,[7] with a lover of hers at my house. She call'd him up stairs, as he was going to Marybone in a hackney-coach.—And I hope, for her own sake and mine, she will perswade the captain to redeem her, for the captain is very generous to the ladies.

LOCKIT. What captain?

TRAPES. He thought I did not know him.—An intimate acquaintance of yours, Mr. Peachum—only Captain Macheath—as fine as a lord.

PEACHUM. To-morrow, dear Mrs. Dye, you shall set your own price upon any of the goods you like—we have at least half a dozen velvet scarfs, and all at your service. Will you give me leave to make you a present of this suit of night-cloaths for your own wearing? —But are you sure it is Captain Macheath?

TRAPES. Though he thinks I have forgot him; no body knows him better. I have taken a great deal of the captain's money in my time at second-hand, for he always lov'd to have his ladies well drest.

PEACHUM. Mr. Lockit and I have a little business with the captain;—you understand me—and we will satisfie you for Mrs. Coaxer's debt.

LOCKIT. Depend upon it—we will deal like men of honour.

TRAPES. I don't enquire after your affairs—so whatever happens, I wash my hands on't.—It hath always

---

[6] customers . . . surgeon's hands either pregnant or being cured of venereal disease [7] shift undergarment, today a slip

been my maxim, that one friend should assist another. —But if you please—I'll take one of the scarfs home with me, 'tis always good to have something in hand.

SCENE VII

Newgate

LUCY

Jealousy, rage, love and fear are at once tearing me to pieces. How I am weather-beaten and shatter'd with distresses!

AIR XLVII. *One evening having lost my way.*

I'm like a skiff on the ocean tost,
Now high, now low, with each billow born,
With her rudder broke, and her anchor lost,
Deserted and all forlorn.
While thus I lye rolling and tossing all night,
That Polly lyes sporting on seas of delight!
Revenge, revenge, revenge,
Shall appease my restless sprite.

I have the rats-bane ready.—I run no risque; for I can lay her death upon the ginn, and so many dye of that naturally that I shall never be call'd in question. —But say I were to be hang'd—I never could be hang'd for any thing that would give me greater comfort, than the poysoning that slut.

(*Enter* FILCH)

FILCH. Madam, here's our Miss Polly come to wait upon you.

LUCY. Show her in.

SCENE VIII

LUCY, POLLY

LUCY. Dear madam, your servant.—I hope you will pardon my passion, when I was so happy to see you last.—I was so over-run with the spleen,[1] that I was perfectly out of my self. And really when one hath the spleen, every thing is to be excus'd by a friend.

AIR XLVIII. *Now Roger, I'll tell thee, because thou'rt my son.*

> When a wife's in her pout,
> (As she's sometimes, no doubt)
> The good husband as meek as a lamb,
> Her vapours to still,
> First grants her her will,
> And the quieting draught is a dram.
> Poor man! And the quieting draught is a dram.

I wish all our quarrels might have so comfortable a reconciliation.

POLLY. I have no excuse for my own behaviour, madam, but my misfortunes.—And really, madam, I suffer too upon your account.

LUCY. But, Miss Polly—in the way of friendship, will you give me leave to propose a glass of cordial to you?

POLLY. Strong-waters are apt to give me the head-ache—I hope, madam, you will excuse me.

LUCY. Not the greatest lady in the land could have better in her closet, for her own private drinking.[2]— You seem mighty low in spirits, my dear.

POLLY. I am sorry, madam, my health will not allow me to accept of your offer.—I should not have left you in the rude manner I did when we met last, madam, had not my papa haul'd me away so unexpectedly.— I was indeed somewhat provok'd, and perhaps might use some expressions that were disrespectful.—But really, madam, the captain treated me with so much contempt and cruelty, that I deserv'd your pity, rather than your resentment.

LUCY. But since his escape, no doubt all matters are made up again.—Ah Polly! Polly! 'tis I am the un-

[1] **spleen** a fit of anger. The spleen was thought to govern the passions and emotions [2] **private drinking** fashionable women professed to drink nothing stronger than wine

happy wife; and he loves you as if you were only his mistress.

POLLY. Sure, madam, you cannot think me so happy as to be the object of your jealousy.—A man is always afraid of a woman who loves him too well—so that I must expect to be neglected and avoided.

LUCY. Then our cases, my dear Polly, are exactly alike. Both of us indeed have been too fond.

AIR XLIX. *O Bessy Bell, etc.*

POLLY. A curse attends that woman's love
  Who always would be pleasing.
LUCY. The pertness of the billing dove,
  Like tickling, is but teazing.

POLLY. What then in love can woman do?
LUCY. If we grow fond they shun us.
POLLY. And when we fly them, they pursue:
LUCY. But leave us when they've won us.

LUCY. Love is so very whimsical in both sexes, that it is impossible to be lasting.—But my heart is particular, and contradicts my own observation.

POLLY. But really, Mistress Lucy, by his last behaviour, I think I ought to envy you.—When I was forc'd from him, he did not shew the least tenderness. —But perhaps, he hath a heart not capable of it.

AIR L. *Wou'd fate to me Belinda give.*

Among the men, coquets we find,
Who court by turns all woman-kind;
And we grant all their hearts desir'd,
When they are flatter'd and admir'd.

The coquets of both sexes are self-lovers, and that is a love no other whatever can dispossess. I fear, my dear Lucy, our husband is one of those.

LUCY. Away with these melancholy reflections,— indeed, my dear Polly, we are both of us a cup too low.—Let me prevail upon you, to accept of my offer.

AIR LI. *Come, sweet lass.*

Come, sweet lass,
Let's banish sorrow
'Till to-morrow;
Come, sweet lass,
Let's take a chirping³ glass.
Wine can clear
The vapours of despair;
And make us light as air;
Then drink, and banish care.

I can't bear, child, to see you in such low spirits.—
And I must persuade you to what I know will do you
good.—I shall now soon be even with the hypocritical
strumpet. (*Aside*)

Scene IX

Polly

All this wheedling of Lucy cannot be for nothing—
At this time too! when I know she hates me!—The dissembling of a woman is always the forerunner of
mischief.—By pouring strong-waters down my throat,
she thinks to pump some secrets out of me—I'll be
upon my guard, and won't taste a drop of her liquor,
I'm resolv'd.

Scene X

Lucy, *with strong-waters,* Polly

Lucy. Come, Miss Polly.
Polly. Indeed, child, you have given yourself
trouble to no purpose.—You must, my dear, excuse me.
Lucy. Really, Miss Polly, you are so squeamishly
affected about taking a cup of strong-waters, as a lady
before company. I vow, Polly, I shall take it mon-
strously ill if you refuse me.—Brandy and men (though

³ **chirping** cheering

women love them never so well) are always taken by us with some reluctance—unless 'tis in private.

POLLY. I protest, madam, it goes against me.—What do I see! Macheath again in custody!—Now every glimmering of happiness is lost. (*Drops the glass of liquor on the ground.*)

LUCY. Since things are thus, I'm glad the wench hath escap'd; for by this event, 'tis plain, she was not happy enough to deserve to be poison'd.

SCENE XI

LOCKIT, MACHEATH, PEACHUM, LUCY, POLLY

LOCKIT. Set your heart to rest, captain.—You have neither the chance of love or money for another escape—for you are order'd to be call'd down upon your tryal immediately.

PEACHUM. Away, hussies!—This is not a time for a man to be hamper'd with his wives.—You see, the gentleman is in chains already.

LUCY. O husband, husband, my heart long'd to see thee; but to see thee thus distracts me!

POLLY. Will not my dear husband look upon his Polly? Why hadst thou not flown to me for protection? with me thou hadst been safe.

AIR LII. *The last time I went o'er the moor.*

POLLY. Hither, dear husband, turn your eyes.
LUCY. Bestow one glance to cheer me.
POLLY. Think with that look, thy Polly dyes.
LUCY. O shun me not,—but hear me.
POLLY. 'Tis Polly sues.
LUCY. —'Tis Lucy speaks.
POLLY. Is thus true love requited?
LUCY. My heart is bursting.
POLLY. —Mine too breaks.
LUCY. Must I,
POLLY. —Must I be slighted?

MACHEATH. What would you have me say, ladies?
—You see, this affair will soon be at an end, without
my disobliging either of you.

PEACHUM. But the settling this point, captain, might
prevent a law-suit between your two widows.

AIR LIII. *Tom Tinker's my true love, etc.*

MACHEATH. Which way shall I turn me—how can I
    decide?
Wives, the day of our death, are as fond as a bride.
One wife is too much for most husbands to hear,
But two at a time there's no mortal can bear.
This way, and that way, and which way I will,
What would comfort the one, t'other wife would take
    ill.

POLLY. But if his own misfortunes have made him
insensible to mine—a father sure will be more compassionate.—Dear, dear sir, sink[1] the material evidence, and bring him off at his tryal—Polly upon her
knees begs it of you.

AIR LIV. *I am a poor shepherd undone.*

When my hero in court appears,
And stands arraign'd for his life,
Then think of poor Polly's tears;
For ah! poor Polly's his wife.
Like the sailor he holds up his hand,
Distrest on the dashing wave.
To die a dry death at land,
Is as bad as a watry grave.
And alas, poor Polly!
Alack, and well-a-day!
Before I was in love,
Oh! every month was May.

LUCY. If Peachum's heart is harden'd; sure you, sir,
will have more compassion on a daughter.—I know
the evidence is in your power.—How then can you
be a tyrant to me?

[1] sink suppress

(*Kneeling*)

AIR LV. *Ianthe the lovely, etc.*

When he holds up his hand arraign'd for his life,
O think of your daughter, and think I'm his wife!
What are cannons, or bombs, or clashing of swords?
For death is more certain by witnesses words.
Then nail up their lips; that dread thunder allay;
And each month of my life will hereafter be May.

LOCKIT. Macheath's time is come, Lucy.—We know our own affairs, therefore let us have no more whimpering or whining.

AIR LVI. *A cobler there was, etc.*

Our selves, like the great, to secure a retreat,
When matters require it, must give up our gang:
And good reasons why,
Or, instead of the fry,[2]
Ev'n Peachum and I,
Like poor petty rascals, might hang, hang;
Like poor petty rascals, might hang.

PEACHUM. Set your heart at rest, Polly.—Your husband is to dye to-day.—Therefore, if you are not already provided, 'tis high time to look about for another. There's comfort for you, you slut.

LOCKIT. We are ready, sir, to conduct you to the Old Baily.

AIR LVII. *Bonny Dundee.*

MACHEATH. The charge is prepar'd; the lawyers are met;
The judges all rang'd (a terrible show!)
I go, undismay'd.—For death is a debt,
A debt on demand.—So, take what I owe.
Then farewell, my love—dear charmers, adieu.
Contented I die—'tis the better for you.
Here ends all dispute the rest of our lives,
For this way at once I please all my wives.

Now, gentlemen, I am ready to attend you.

[2] **fry** small fry

Scene XII

Lucy, Polly, Filch

Polly. Follow them, Filch, to the court. And when the tryal is over, bring me a particular account of his behaviour, and of every thing that happen'd.—You'll find me here with Miss Lucy. (*Exeunt* Filch) But why is all this musick?

Lucy. The prisoners, whose tryals are put off till next Session, are diverting themselves.

Polly. Sure there is nothing so charming as musick! I'm fond of it to distraction—But alas!—now, all mirth seems an insult upon my affliction.—Let us retire, my dear Lucy, and indulge our sorrows.—The noisy crew, you see, are coming upon us.

(*Exeunt*)

(*A dance of prisoners in chains, etc.*)

Scene XIII

The condemn'd hold

Macheath, *in a melancholy posture*

air LVIII. *Happy groves.*

O cruel, cruel, cruel case!
Must I suffer this disgrace?

air LIX. *Of all the girls that are so smart.*

Of all the friends in time of grief,
When threatning death looks grimmer,
Not one so sure can bring relief,
As this best friend a brimmer.[1]   (*Drinks*)

air LX. *Britons strike home.*

Since I must swing,—I scorn, I scorn to wince or
whine.   (*Rises*)

[1] **brimmer** a cup, brimful

AIR LXI. *Chevy Chase.*

But now again my spirits sink;
I'll raise them high with wine. (*Drinks a glass of wine*)

AIR LXII. *To old Sir Simon the king.*

But valour the stronger grows,
The stronger liquor we're drinking.
And how can we feel our woes,
When we've lost the trouble of thinking?   (*Drinks*)

AIR LXIII. *Joy to great Caesar.*

If thus—A man can die
Much bolder with brandy.
              (*Pours out a bumper of brandy*)

AIR LXIV. *There was an old woman, etc.*

So I drink off this bumper—And now I can stand the
    test,
And my comrades shall see, that I die as brave as the
    best.   (*Drinks*)

AIR LXV. *Did you ever hear of a gallant sailor.*

But can I leave my pretty hussies,
Without one tear, or tender sigh?

AIR LXVI. *Why are mine eyes still flowing.*

Their eyes, their lips, their busses[2]
Recall my love—Ah must I die!

AIR LXVII. *Green sleeves.*

Since laws were made for ev'ry degree,
To curb vice in others, as well as me,
I wonder we han't better company
Upon Tyburn tree!
But gold from law can take out the sting;
And if rich men like us were to swing,
'Twou'd thin the land, such numbers to string
Upon Tyburn tree!

---

[2] busses kisses

JAILOR. Some friends of yours, captain, desire to be admitted—I leave you together.

SCENE XIV

MACHEATH, BEN BUDGE, MATT OF THE MINT

MACHEATH. For my having broke prison, you see, gentlemen, I am order'd immediate execution.—The sheriff's officers, I believe, are now at the door.—That Jemmy Twitcher should peach me, I own surpriz'd me!—'Tis a plain proof that the world is all alike, and that even our gang can no more trust one another than other people. Therefore, I beg you, gentlemen, look well to your selves, for in all probability you may live some months longer.

MATT. We are heartily sorry, captain, for your misfortune.—But 'tis what we must all come to.

MACHEATH. Peachum and Lockit, you know, are infamous scoundrels. Their lives are as much in your power, as yours are in theirs—Remember your dying friend!—'Tis my last request.—Bring those villains to the gallows before you, and I am satisfied.

MATT. We'll do't.

JAILOR. Miss Polly and Miss Lucy intreat a word with you.

MACHEATH. Gentlemen, adieu.

SCENE XV

LUCY, MACHEATH, POLLY

MACHEATH. My dear Lucy—my dear Polly—Whatsoever hath past between us is now at an end.—If you are fond of marrying again, the best advice I can give you, is to ship yourselves off for the West-Indies, where you'll have a fair chance of getting a husband a-piece; or by good luck, two or three, as you like best.[1]

POLLY. How can I support this sight!

[1] Transported felons often remained in the colonies after completing their sentences, and wives were thus at a premium

LUCY. There is nothing moves one so much as a great man in distress.

AIR LXVIII. *All you that must take a leap, etc.*

LUCY. Would I might be hang'd!
POLLY. —And I would so too!
LUCY. To be hang'd with you,
POLLY. —My dear, with you.
MACHEATH. O leave me to thought! I fear! I doubt!
I tremble! I droop!—See, my courage is out.
                    (*Turns up the empty bottle*)
POLLY. No token of love?
MACHEATH. —See, my courage is out.
                    (*Turns up the empty pot*)
LUCY. No token of love?
POLLY. —Adieu.
LUCY. —Farewell.
MACHEATH. But hark! I hear the toll of the bell.
CHORUS. Tol de rol lol, etc.

JAILOR. Four women more, captain, with a child a-piece! See, here they come.

(*Enter women and children*)

MACHEATH. What—four wives more!—This is too much.—Here—tell the sheriff's officers I am ready. (*Exit* MACHEATH *guarded*)

SCENE XVI

To them, enter PLAYER *and* BEGGAR

PLAYER. But, honest friend, I hope you don't intend that Macheath shall be really executed.

BEGGAR. Most certainly, sir.—To make the piece perfect, I was for doing strict poetical justice.— Macheath is to be hang'd; and for the other personages of the drama, the audience must have suppos'd they were all either hang'd or transported.

PLAYER. Why then, friend, this is a down-right deep tragedy. The catastrophe is manifestly wrong, for an opera must end happily.

BEGGAR. Your objection, sir, is very just; and is easily remov'd. For you must allow, that in this kind of drama, 'tis no matter how absurdly things are brought about—So—you rabble there—run and cry a reprieve —let the prisoner be brought back to his wives in triumph.

PLAYER. All this we must do, to comply with the taste of the town.[1]

BEGGAR. Through the whole piece, you may observe such a similitude of manners in high and low life, that it is difficult to determine whether (in the fashionable vices) the fine gentlemen imitate the gentlemen of the road, or the gentlemen of the road the fine gentlemen. —Had the play remain'd, as I at first intended, it would have carried a most excellent moral. 'Twould have shown that the lower sort of people have their vices in a degree as well as the rich: And that they are punish'd for them.

SCENE XVII

To them MACHEATH with rabble, etc.

MACHEATH. So, it seems, I am not left to my choice, but must have a wife at last.—Look ye, my dears, we will have no controversie now. Let us give this day to mirth, and I am sure she who thinks her self my wife will testifie her joy by a dance.

ALL. Come, a dance—a dance.

MACHEATH. Ladies, I hope you will give me leave to present a partner to each of you. And (if I may without offence) for this time, I take Polly for mine. —And for life, you slut,—for we were really marry'd.— As for the rest.—But at present keep your own secret. (To Polly)

---

[1] Macheath's outlandish reprieve satirizes the unmotivated and unnatural endings of the Italian opera and of the sentimental comedy

A *dance*

AIR LXIX. *Lumps of pudding, etc.*

Thus I stand like the Turk, with his doxies around;
From all sides their glances his passion confound;
For black, brown, and fair, his inconstancy burns,
And the different beauties subdue him by turns:
Each calls forth her charms, to provoke his desires:
Though willing to all; with but one he retires.
But think of this maxim, and put off your sorrow,
The wretch of to-day, may be happy to-morrow.
CHORUS. But think of this maxim, etc.

FINIS.

From TRIVIA *

Through winter streets to steer your course aright,
How to walk clean by day, and safe by night,
How jostling crouds with prudence to decline,
When to assert the wall,[2] and when resign,
I sing:[3] Thou, *Trivia, goddess*, aid my song,
Thro' spacious streets conduct thy bard along;
By thee transported, I securely stray
Where winding alleys lead the doubtful [4] way,
The silent court and op'ning square explore,
10 And long perplexing lanes, untrod before.
To pave thy realm, and smooth the broken ways,
Earth from her womb a flinty tribute pays;[5]
For thee, the sturdy paver thumps the ground,
Whilst ev'ry stroke his lab'ring lungs resound;
For thee the scavinger bids kennels[6] glide
Within their bounds, and heaps of dirt subside.
My youthful bosom burns with thirst of fame,
From the great theme to build a glorious name,
To tread in paths to ancient bards unknown,
20 And bind my temples with a civic crown;
But more, my country's love demands the lays,
My country's be the profit, mine the praise.

* *Trivia* (1716), patterned roughly on Virgil's *Georgics*, is a
burlesque how-to-do treatise on "The Art of Walking the Streets
of London" (Gay's subtitle). The poem reveals Gay's extraordinary knowledge of the city and especially its underworld, a
knowledge which served him well later in *The Beggar's Opera*
[2] wall in Gay's London it was advisable to walk next to the
buildings ("wall") to avoid the dirt and refuse in the streets
[3] a parody of the conventional invocation to the Muse. In Roman
mythology, the title, Trivia, "goddess of the crossroads," was
often applied to Diana [4] doubtful unfamiliar [5] Earth . . .
pays paving flints or stones [6] kennels gutters

• • • • •

O happy streets, to rumbling wheels unknown,
No carts, no coaches shake the floating town! [7]
Thus was of old *Britannia*'s city bless'd,
E'er pride and luxury her sons possess'd:
Coaches and chariots yet unfashion'd lay,
Nor late-invented chairs perplex'd the way:
Then the proud lady trip'd along the town,
And tuck'd up petticoats secur'd her gown,   30
Her rosy cheek with distant visits glow'd
And exercise unartful charms bestow'd;
But since in braided gold her foot is bound,
And a long trailing manteau sweeps the ground,
Her shoe disdains the street; the lazy fair
With narrow step affects a limping air.
Now gaudy pride corrupts the lavish age,
And the streets flame with glaring equipage;
The tricking gamester insolently rides,
With *Loves* and *Graces*[8] on his chariot's sides;   40
In saucy state the griping broker sits,
And laughs at honesty, and trudging wits:
For you, O honest men, these useful lays
The muse prepares; I seek no other praise.

• • • • •

Where fam'd *St. Giles*'s ancient limits spread,
An inrail'd column rears its lofty head,
Here to sev'n streets sev'n dials count the day,
And from each other catch the circling ray.
Here oft the peasant, with enquiring face,
Bewilder'd, trudges on from place to place;   50
He dwells on ev'ry sign[9] with stupid gaze,

---

[7] **floating town** Gay has just finished describing Venice [8] **Loves and Graces** Cupids and other ornamental figures [9] Street numbers were unknown in Gay's time and shops were identified by signs illustrating the merchandise sold or service performed

Enters the narrow alley's doubtful maze,
Tries ev'ry winding court and street in vain,
And doubles o'er his weary steps again.
Thus hardy *Theseus* with intrepid feet,
Travers'd the dang'rous labyrinth of *Crete;*
But still the wandring passes forc'd his stay,
Till *Ariadne*'s clue unwinds the way.
But do not thou, like that bold chief, confide
60 Thy ventrous[10] footsteps to a female guide;
She'll lead thee with delusive smiles along,
Dive in thy fob,[11] and drop thee in the throng.

• • • • •

Where elevated o'er the gaping croud,
Clasp'd in the board the perjur'd head is bow'd,
Betimes retreat; here, thick as hailstones, pour
Turnips, and half-hatch'd eggs (a mingled show'r)
Among the rabble rain: Some random throw
May with the trickling yolk thy cheek o'erflow.
Though expedition bids, yet never stray
70 Where no rang'd posts defend the rugged way.
Here laden carts with thund'ring waggons meet,
Wheels clash with wheels, and bar the narrow street;
The lashing whip resounds, the horses strain,
And blood in anguish bursts the swelling vein.
O barb'rous men, your cruel breasts assuage,
Why vent ye on the gen'rous steed your rage?
Does not his service earn your daily bread?
Your wives, your children, by his labours fed!
If, as the *Samian*[12] taught, the soul revives,
80 And, shifting seats, in other bodies lives;
Severe shall be the brutal coachman's change,
Doom'd in a hackney horse the town to range:
Carmen, transform'd, the groaning load shall draw,

---

[10] **ventrous** venturous   [11] **fob** watch pocket; see also Jenny Diver
in *The Beggar's Opera*   [12] **Samian** Pythagoras, who taught the
transmigration of souls

Whom other tyrants with the lash shall awe.
Who would of *Watlingstreet* the dangers share,
When the broad pavement of *Cheapside* is near?
Or who that rugged street would traverse o'er,
That stretches, O *Fleet-ditch*, from thy black shore
To the *Tow'r's* moated walls? [13] Here steams ascend
That, in mix'd fumes, the wrinkled nose offend.   90
Where chandlers[14] cauldrons boil; where fishy prey
Hide the wet stall, long absent from the sea;
And where the cleaver chops the heifer's spoil,
And where huge hogsheads sweat with trainy oil,[15]
The breathing nostril hold; but how shall I
Pass, where in piles *Cornavian*[16] cheeses lie;
Cheese, that the table's closing rites denies,
And bids me with th' unwilling chaplain rise.[17]

· · · · ·

But sometimes let me leave the noisy roads,
And silent wander in the close abodes   100
Where wheels ne'er shake the ground; there pensive
    stray,
In studious thought, the long uncrouded way.
Here I remark each walker's diff'rent face,
And in their look their various bus'ness trace.
The broker here his spacious beaver wears,
Upon his brow sit jealousies and cares;
Bent on some mortgage (to avoid reproach)
He seeks bye streets, and saves th' expensive coach.
Soft, at low doors, old letchers tap their cane,
For fair recluse, who travels *Drury-lane;*   110
Here roams uncomb'd the lavish rake, to shun
His *Fleetstreet* draper's[18] everlasting dun.
Careful observers, studious of the town,

---

[13] street . . . walls Thames Street ran from Blackfriars, where
Fleet Ditch emptied into the Thames, to the Tower of London
[14] chandlers candle makers   [15] trainy oil fish oil, especially whale
or cod   [16] Cornavian Cheshire anciently so called (Gay's note)
[17] cheese . . . rise before dessert   [18] draper's tailor's

Shun the misfortunes that disgrace the clown;[19]
Untempted, they contemn the jugler's feats,
Pass by the *Meuse*,[20] nor try the thimble's cheats.[21]
When drays bound high, they never cross behind,
Where bubbling yeast is blown by gusts of wind:
And when up *Ludgate-hill* huge carts move slow,
120 Far from the straining steeds securely go,
Whose dashing hoofs behind them fling the mire,
And mark with muddy blots the gazing 'squire.

     •   •   •   •   •

     Where *Covent-garden*'s famous temple stands,
That boasts the work of *Jones'* immortal hands,[22]
Columns with plain magnificence appear,
And graceful porches lead along the square:
Here oft my course I bend, when lo! from far
I spy the furies of the foot-ball war:
The 'prentice quits his shop to join the crew,
130 Encreasing crouds the flying game pursue.
Thus, as you roll the ball o'er snowy ground,
The gath'ring globe augments with ev'ry round,
But whither shall I run? the throng draws nigh,
The ball now skims the street, now soars on high;
The dext'rous glazier strong returns the bound,
And jingling sashes on the pent-house[23] sound.

     •   •   •   •   •

     Experienc'd men, inur'd to city ways,
Need not the calendar to count their days.
When thro' the town with slow and solemn air,
140 Led by the nostril, walks the muzzled bear;

[19] **clown** rustic   [20] **Meuse** the Mews, near Charing Cross, originally the King's stables; an area frequented by gamblers and swindlers   [21] **thimble's cheats** the shell game   [22] **Where . . . hands** St. Paul's Church, Covent Garden, was designed by the famous seventeenth-century architect, Inigo Jones   [23] **pent-house** structure built on the roof to cover a stairway or ventilating shaft

Behind him moves majestically dull,
The pride of *Hockley hole*,[24] the surly bull;
Learn hence the periods of the week to name,
Mondays and *Thursdays* are the days of game.

When fishy stalls with double store are laid;
The golden-belly'd carp, the broad-finn'd maid,[25]
Red-speckled trouts, the salmon's silver jowl,
The jointed lobster, and unscaly sole,
And luscious 'scallops, to allure the tastes
Of rigid zealots to delicious fasts;   150
Wednesdays and *Fridays* you'll observe from hence,
Days, when our sires were doom'd to abstinence.

When dirty waters from balconies drop,
And dext'rous damsels twirle the sprinkling mop,
And cleanse the spatter'd sash, and scrub the stairs;
Know *Saturday*'s conclusive morn appears.

Successive crys the seasons change declare,
And mark the monthly progress of the year.
Hark, how the streets with treble voices ring,
To sell the bounteous product of the spring!   160
Sweet-smelling flow'rs, and elder's early bud,
With nettle's tender shoots, to cleanse the blood:
And when *June*'s thunder cools the sultry skies,
Ev'n *Sundays* are prophan'd by mackrel cries.

Wallnuts the fruit'rer's hand, in autumn, stain,
Blue plumbs and juicy pears augment his gain;
Next oranges the longing boys entice,
To trust their copper fortunes to the dice.

• • • • •

Come F——[26] sincere, experienc'd friend,   170
Thy briefs, thy deeds, and ev'n thy fees suspend;
Come let us leave the *Temple*'s[27] silent walls,
Me bus'ness to my distant lodging calls:

[24] **Hockley hole** see p. 13, n. 3   [25] **maid** a young ray or skate
[26] **F——** William Fortescue, an attorney of the Inner Temple,
Gay's boyhood friend   [27] **Temple** see p. 11, n. 3

Thro' the long *Strand* together let us stray:
With thee conversing, I forget the way.[28]
Behold that narrow street which steep descends,
Whose building to the slimy shore extends;
Here *Arundel*'s fam'd structure[29] rear'd its frame,
The street alone retains an empty name:
Where *Titian*'s glowing paint the canvas warm'd,
180 And *Raphael*'s fair design, with judgment charm'd,
Now hangs the bell-man's song,[30] and pasted here
The colour'd prints of *Overton*[31] appear.
Where statues breath'd, the work of *Phidias*' hands,
A wooden pump, or lonely watch-house stands.
There *Essex*' stately pile adorn'd the shore,
There *Cecil*'s, *Bedford*'s, *Villers*',[32] now no more.
Yet *Burlington*'s fair palace[33] still remains;
Beauty within, without proportion reigns.
Beneath his eye declining art revives,
190 The wall with animated picture lives;
There *Hendel* strikes the strings,[34] the melting strain
Transports the soul, and thrills thro' ev'ry vein;
There oft I enter (but with cleaner shoes)
For *Burlington*'s belov'd by ev'ry Muse.

• • • • •

Where the mob gathers, swiftly shoot along,
Nor idly mingle in the noisy throng:
Lur'd by the silver hilt, amid the swarm,

[28] **With thee . . . way** an echo of Milton's "With thee conversing I forget all time," *Paradise Lost*, IV, 639 [29] **Arundel's . . . structure** Arundel House, in the Strand, famous for its art collection. In Gay's time only the name Arundel Street served as a reminder of the once great showplace [30] **bell-man's song** the watchman often blessed the sleeping houses in verse as he passed [31] **Overton** a well known dealer in prints and engravings [32] **Essex . . . Cecil's, Bedford's, Villers'** Essex House, Cecil House, Bedford House, York House, town residences of some of England's great families [33] **Burlington's . . . palace** Burlington House, Piccadilly, residence of Robert Boyle, Earl of Burlington and Gay's patron [34] **Hendel . . . strings** Handel occupied an apartment in Burlington House from 1715 to 1718

The subtil artist will thy side disarm.
Nor is thy flaxen wig with safety worn;
High on the shoulder, in a basket born   200
Lurks the sly boy; whose hand to rapine bred,
Plucks off the curling honours of thy head.
Here dives the skulking thief with practis'd sleight,
And unfelt fingers make thy pocket light.
Where's now thy watch, with all its trinkets, flown?
And thy late snuff-box is no more thy own.
But lo! his bolder theft some tradesman spies,
Swift from his prey the scudding[35] lurcher flies;
Dext'rous he 'scapes the coach with nimble bounds,
Whilst ev'ry honest tongue *stop thief* resounds.   210
So speeds the wily fox, alarm'd by fear,
Who lately filch'd the turkey's callow care;
Hounds following hounds grow louder as he flies,
And injur'd tenants join the hunter's cries.
Breathless he stumbling falls: Ill-fated boy!
Why did not honest work thy youth employ?
Seiz'd by rough hands, he's dragg'd amid the rout,
And stretch'd beneath the pump's incessant spout:
Or plung'd in miry ponds, he gasping lies,
Mud chokes his mouth, and plaisters o'er his eyes.   220
   Let not the ballad-singer's shrilling strain
Amid the swarm thy list'ning ear detain:
Guard well thy pocket; for these *Syrens* stand
To aid the labours of the diving hand;
Confed'rate in the cheat, they draw the throng,
And cambrick handkerchiefs reward the song.

· · · · ·

Where *Lincoln's-Inn's*[36] wide space is rail'd around,
Cross not with vent'rous step; there oft is found
The lurking thief, who while the day-light shone,

[35] **scudding** running swiftly   [36] **Lincoln's-Inn's** Lincoln's Inn
Fields, haunt of thieves and cutthroats; after 1714, the site of
the Theatre Royal where *The Beggar's Opera* was first performed

230 Made the walls echo with his begging tone:
That crutch which late compassion mov'd shall wound
Thy bleeding head, and fell thee to the ground.
Tho' thou are tempted by the link-man's[37] call,
Yet trust him not along the lonely wall;
In the mid-way he'll quench the flaming brand,
And share the booty with the pilf'ring band.
Still keep the publick streets, where oily rays
Shot from the crystal lamp, o'erspread the ways.

• • • • •

Who can the various city frauds recite,
240 With all the petty rapines of the night?
Who now the guinea-dropper's[38] bait regards,
Trick'd by the sharper's dice, or juggler's cards?
Why should I warn thee ne'er to join the fray,
Where the sham quarrel interrupts the way?
Lives there in these our days so soft a clown,
Brav'd by the bully's oaths, or threat'ning frown?
I need not strict enjoin the pocket's care,
When from the crouded play you lead the fair;
Who has not here, or watch, or snuff-box lost,[39]
250 Or handkerchiefs that *India*'s shuttle boast.
O! may thy virtue guard thee thro' the roads
Of *Drury*'s mazy courts, and dark abodes,
The harlot's guileful paths, who nightly stand,
Where *Katherinestreet* descends into the *Strand*.
Say, vagrant Muse, their wiles and subtil arts,
To lure the strangers unsuspecting hearts;
So shall our youth on healthful sinews tread,
And city cheeks grow warm with rural red.
'Tis she who nightly strolls with saunt'ring pace,
260 No stubborn stays her yielding shape embrace;
Beneath the lamp her tawdry ribbons glare,
The new-scour'd manteau, and the slattern air;

---

[37] link-man a public torch bearer, available for hire [38] guinea-dropper one who attracts a gambling victim by dropping a guinea and offering to share [39] or . . . or either . . . or

High-draggled petticoats her travels show,
And hollow cheeks with artful blushes glow;
With flatt'ring sounds she sooths the cred'lous ear,
My noble captain! charmer! love! my dear!
In riding-hood near tavern doors she plies,
Or muffled pinners[40] hide her livid eyes.
With empty bandbox she delights to range,
And feigns a distant errand from the *'Change;*[41]   270
Nay, she will oft the Quaker's hood profane,
And trudge demure the rounds of *Drury-lane.*
She darts from sarsnet[42] ambush wily leers,
Twitches thy sleeve, or with familiar airs
Her fan will pat thy cheek; these snares disdain,
Nor gaze behind thee, when she turns again.
   I knew a yeoman, who for thirst of gain,
To the great city drove from *Devon*'s plain
His num'rous lowing herd; his herds he sold,
And his deep leathern pocket bagg'd with gold;   280
Drawn by a fraudful nymph, he gaz'd, he sigh'd;
Unmindful of his home, and distant bride,
She leads the willing victim to his doom,
Through winding alleys to her cobweb room.
Thence thro' the street he reels from post to post,
Valiant with wine, nor knows his treasure lost.
The vagrant wretch th' assembled watchmen spies,
He waves his hanger,[43] and their poles defies;
Deep in the Round-house[44] pent, all night he snores,
And the next morn in vain his fate deplores.   290
   Ah hapless swain, unus'd to pains and ills!
Canst thou forego roast beef for nauseous pills?
How wilt thou lift to Heav'n thy eyes and hands,
When the long scroll the surgeon's fees demands!
Or else (ye Gods avert that worst disgrace)
Thy ruin'd nose falls level with thy face;
Then shall thy wife thy loathsome kiss disdain,

[40] **pinners** a woman's cap which covered the sides of the face
[41] **'Change** Exchange, in the Strand, London's chief shopping
center   [42] **sarsnet** sarcenet, a soft silk fabric   [43] **hanger** short
sword   [44] **Round-house** constable's jail

And wholesome neighbours from thy mug refrain.
   Yet there are watchmen, who with friendly light
300 Will teach thy reeling steps to tread aright;
For sixpence will support thy helpless arm,
And home conduct thee, safe from nightly harm;
But if they shake their lanthorns, from afar
To call their brethren to confed'rate war
When rakes resist their power; if hapless you
Should chance to wander with the scow'ring crew;[45]
Tho' fortune yield thee captive, ne'er despair,
But seek the constable's consid'rate ear;
He will reverse the watchman's harsh decree,
310 Mov'd by the rhet'rick of a silver fee.
Thus would you gain some fav'rite courtier's word;
Fee not the petty clerks, but bribe my Lord.

[45] **scow'ring crew** street brawlers

NEWGATE'S GARLAND *

❧

I.

Ye gallants of *Newgate*, whose fingers are nice,
In diving in pockets, or cogging² of dice.
Ye sharpers so rich, who can buy off the noose,
Ye honester poor rogues, who die in your shoes,
Attend and draw near,
Good news ye shall hear,
How *Jonathan's* throat was cut from ear to ear;
How *Blueskin's³* sharp penknife hath set you at ease,
And every man round me may rob, if he please.

II.

When to the *Old-Bailey* this *Blueskin* was led,   10
He held up his hand, his indictment was read,
Loud rattled his chains, near him *Jonathan* stood,
For full forty pounds was the price of his blood.
Then hopeless of life,
He drew his penknife,
And made a sad widow of *Jonathan's* wife.
But forty pounds paid her, her grief shall appease,
And every man round me may rob, if he please.

* Based on the sensational proceedings during the trial of three
notorious highwaymen, Jonathan Wild, Jonathan Blake, and
Jack Sheppard, in 1724. Wild, London's master criminal who
turned King's evidence, was attacked and nearly killed while
visiting Blake in his cell. The ballad's ties with *The Beggar's
Opera* are many: the Newgate setting; Wild as the prototype
for Peachum; the similarity in tone between *Newgate's Garland*
and many of the airs in the play; the parallel drawn between
cutthroat and courtier   ² **cogging** cheating   ³ **Blueskin** Blake's
nickname

III.

Some say there are courtiers of highest renown,
Who steal the King's gold, and leave him but a
20   Crown;[4]
Some say there are peers, and some Parliament men,
Who meet once a year to rob courtiers agen: [5]
Let them all take their swing,
To pillage the King,
And get a blue ribbon[6] instead of a string.
Now *Blueskin*'s sharp penknife hath set you at ease,
And every man round me may rob, if he please.

IV.

Knaves of old, to hide guilt by their cunning inven-
     tions,
Call'd briberies grants, and plain robberies pensions;
30 Physicians and lawyers (who take their degrees
To be learned rogues) call'd their pilfering, fees;
Since this happy day,
Now ev'ry man may
Rob (as safe as in office) upon the highway.
For *Blueskin*'s sharp penknife hath set you at ease,
And every man round me may rob, if he please.

V.

Some cheat in the Customs, some rob the Excise,[7]
But he who robs both is esteemed most wise.
Church-wardens, too prudent to hazard the halter,
40 As yet only venture to steal from the altar:
But now to get gold,
They may be more bold,
And rob on the highway, since *Jonathan*'s cold.
For *Blueskin*'s sharp penknife hath set you at ease,
And every man round me may rob, if he please.

[4] **Crown** with a pun on Crown (diadem) and Crown (coin)
[5] **agen** in turn   [6] **blue ribbon** Order of the Garter   [7] **Excise** Tax Office

VI.

Some by publick revenues, which pass'd through their
    hands,
Have purchas'd clean houses, and bought dirty lands,
Some to steal from a charity think it no sin,
Which, at home (says the proverb) does always begin;
But, if ever you be   50
Assign'd a trustee,
Treat not orphans like Masters of the Chancery,[8]
But take the highway, and more honestly seize,
For every man round me may rob, if he please.

VII.

What a pother has here been with *Wood* and his
    brass,[9]
Who would modestly make a few half-pennies pass?
The patent is good, and the precedent's old,
For *Diomede* changed his copper for gold:[10]
But, if *Ireland* despise
Thy new half-pennies,   60
With more safety to rob on the road I advise.
For *Blueskin*'s sharp penknife has set thee at ease,
And ev'ry man round me may rob, if he please.

[8] **Masters . . . Chancery** court appointed trustees of minors'
estates who were often notoriously dishonest [9] **Wood . . .
brass** William Wood was granted a patent in 1724 to manufac-
ture copper halfpence for use in Ireland. Swift, in the *Drapier's
Letters* exposed the fraudulent nature of the new mintage
[10] **Diomede . . . gold** *Iliad*, VI, 232-36. Diomede and Glaucus
exchanged armor on the battlefield and Diomede got golden
armor in exchange for his bronze, or copper. I am indebted to
Professor Charles Beckwith for identifying the allusion

'TWAS WHEN THE SEAS
WERE ROARING. A BALLAD *

I.

'Twas when the seas were roaring
With hollow blasts of wind;
A damsel lay deploring,
All on a rock reclin'd.
Wide o'er the rolling billows
She cast a wistful look;
Her head was crown'd with willows
That tremble o'er the brook.

II.

Twelve months are gone and over,
And nine long tedious days.
Why didst thou, vent'rous lover,
Why didst thou trust the seas?
Cease, cease, thou cruel ocean,
And let my lover rest:
Ah! what's thy troubled motion
To that within my breast?

III.

The merchant, rob'd of pleasure,
Sees tempests in despair;

10

* From Gay's play, *The What D'ye Call It* (1715). The music,
by Handel, was used again for Air XXVIII ("How cruel are
the traytors") of *The Beggar's Opera*. This piece, together with
Sweet William's Farewell (1720) and *Molly Mog* (1726), reveals Gay's lyric talent, somewhat rare in Augustan poetry, and
his early interest in the ballad

88

But what's the loss of treasure
To losing of my dear?   20
Should you some coast be laid on
Where gold and di'monds grow,
You'd find a richer maiden,
But none that loves you so.

IV.

How can they say that nature
Has nothing made in vain;
Why then beneath the water
Should hideous rocks remain?
No eyes the rocks discover,
That lurk beneath the deep,   30
To wreck the wand'ring lover,
And leave the maid to weep.[2]

V.

All melancholy lying,
Thus wail'd she for her dear;
Repay'd each blast with sighing,
Each billow with a tear;
When, o'er the white wave stooping,
His floating corpse she spy'd;
Then like a lilly drooping,
She bow'd her head, and dy'd.   40

[2] Stanza IV parallels closely Dorigen's lament in Chaucer's "The
Franklin's Tale"

SWEET WILLIAM'S FAREWELL
TO BLACK-EY'D SUSAN. A BALLAD *

I.

All in the *Downs*[2] the fleet was moor'd,
The streamers waving in the wind,
When black-ey'd *Susan* came aboard.
Oh! where shall I my true love find!
Tell me, ye jovial sailors, tell me true,
If my sweet *William* sails among the crew.

II.

William, who high upon the yard,[3]
Rock'd with the billow to and fro,
Soon as her well-known voice he heard,
10   He sigh'd, and cast his eyes below:
The cord slides swiftly through his glowing hands,
And, (quick as lightning,) on the deck he stands.

III.

So the sweet lark, high-pois'd in air,
Shuts close his pinions to his breast,
(If, chance, his mate's shrill call he hear)
And drops at once into her nest.
The noblest captain in the *British* fleet,
Might envy *William*'s lip those kisses sweet.

* The music for this ballad was later used for Air XXXIV ("Thus
when the swallow seeking prey") of *The Beggar's Opera*
[2] **Downs** roadstead in the English Channel off the coast of Kent
[3] **yard** yardarm

IV.

O *Susan, Susan,* lovely dear,
My vows shall ever true remain;   20
Let me kiss off that falling tear,
We only part to meet again.
Change, as ye list, ye winds; my heart shall be
The faithful compass that still points to thee.

V.

Believe not what the landmen say,
Who tempt with doubts thy constant mind:
They'll tell thee, sailors, when away,
In ev'ry port a mistress find.
Yes, yes, believe them when they tell thee so,
For thou art present wheresoe'er I go.   30

VI.

If to far *India's* coast we sail,
Thy eyes are seen in di'monds bright,
Thy breath is *Africk's* spicy gale,
Thy skin is ivory, so white.
Thus ev'ry beauteous object that I view,
Wakes in my soul some charm of lovely *Sue*.

VII.

Though battel call me from thy arms,
Let not my pretty *Susan* mourn;
Though cannons roar, yet safe from harms,
William shall to his dear return.   40
Love turns aside the balls that round me fly,
Lest precious tears should drop from *Susan's* eye.

VIII.

The boatswain gave the dreadful word,
The sails their swelling bosom spread,

No longer must she stay aboard:
They kiss'd, she sigh'd, he hung his head.
Her less'ning boat, unwilling rows to land:
Adieu, she cries! and wav'd her lilly hand.

MOLLY MOG: OR, THE FAIR MAID OF THE INN *

Says my Uncle, I pray you discover
What hath been the cause of your woes,
Why you pine, and you whine, like a lover?
I have seen *Molly Mog* of the *Rose*.

O Nephew! your grief is but folly,
In town you may find better prog;[2]
Half a crown there will get you a *Molly*,[3]
A *Molly* much better than *Mog*.

I know that by Wits 'tis recited,
That women at best are a clog;[4]   10
But I am not so easily frighted,
From loving of sweet *Molly Mog*.

The school-boy's desire is a play-day,
The school-master's joy is to flog;
The milk-maid's delight is on *May-Day*,
But mine is on sweet *Molly Mog*.

Will-a-wisp leads the trav'ler a gadding
Thro' ditch, and thro' quagmire and bog;
But no light can set me a madding,
Like the eyes of my sweet *Molly Mog*.   20

* according to a note accompanying the poem on its first appearance in 1726, Molly Mog was the attractive daughter of the host at the Rose Inn in Wokingham, Berkshire, where "two or three Men of Wit" stayed overnight. The trio was most likely Pope, Swift, and Gay and the poem, a collaboration   [2] **prog** food usually obtained by foraging or as a handout. The three poets were obviously hard pressed for rhymes   [3] **Molly** here slang, meaning "moll," a prostitute   [4] **clog** encumbrance

For guineas in other men's breeches
Your gamesters will palm and will cog;
But I envy them none of their riches,
So I may win sweet *Molly Mog*.

The heart,[5] when half-wounded, is changing,
It here and there leaps like a frog;
But my heart can never be ranging,
'Tis so fix'd upon sweet *Molly Mog*.

Who follows all ladies of pleasure,
30 In pleasure is thought but a hog:
All the sex cannot give so good measure
Of joys, as my sweet *Molly Mog*.

I feel I'm in love to distraction,
My senses all lost in a fog;
And nothing can give satisfaction
But thinking of sweet *Molly Mog*.

A letter when I am inditing,
Comes *Cupid* and gives me a jog,
And I fill all the paper with writing
40 Of nothing but sweet *Molly Mog*.

If I would not give up the three *Graces*[6]
I wish I were hang'd like a dog,
And at Court all the drawing-room faces,
For a glance of my sweet *Molly Mog*.

Those faces want[7] nature and spirit,
And seem as cut out of a log;
Juno, *Venus*, and *Pallas*'s merit
Unite in my sweet *Molly Mog*.

Those who toast all the Family Royal,
50 In bumpers of hogan and nog,[8]

---

[5] **heart** with a pun on "hart"   [6] **Graces** in mythology, the three beautiful sisters who attended the Muses   [7] **want** lack [8] **hogan and nog** strong liquor and a type of heady ale

Have hearts not more true or more loyal
Than mine to my sweet *Molly Mog*.

Were *Virgil* alive with his *Phillis*,
And writing another eclogue;
Both his *Phillis* and fair *Amaryllis*
He'd give up for sweet *Molly Mog*.

When she smiles on each guest, like her liquor,
Then jealousy sets me agog.
To be sure she's a bit for the *Vicar*,
And so I shall lose *Molly Mog*.   60

AN EPISTLE TO A LADY *

Madam, to all your censures I submit,
And frankly own I should long since have writ:
You told me, silence would be thought a crime,
And kindly strove to teaze me into rhyme:
No more let trifling themes your Muse employ,
Nor lavish verse to paint a female toy:[2]
No more on plains with rural damsels sport,[3]
But sing the glories of the *British* court.
    By your commands and inclination sway'd,
10 I call'd th' unwilling Muses to my aid;
Resolv'd to write, the noble theme I chose,
And to the Princess thus the poem rose.

Aid me, bright Phoebus; *aid, ye sacred Nine;*[4]
Exalt my genius, and my verse refine.
My strains with Carolina's *name I grace,*
The lovely parent of our royal race.
Breathe soft, ye winds, ye waves in silence sleep;
Let prosp'rous breezes wanton o'er the deep,
Swell the white sails, and with the streamers play,
20 *To waft her gently o'er the watry way.*

    Here I to *Neptune* form'd a pompous pray'r,
To rein the winds, and guard the royal fair;[5]

---

* Addressed to the Princess Caroline of Ansbach (the future
Queen Caroline) on her arrival in England in October, 1714.
Gay had met the Princess that summer in Hanover and the
Epistle, a lavish poetic reminder of his presence and of his hopes
for a place at Court, is early evidence of his involvement with
the world of Whitehall and St. James's [2] **toy** Gay's poem, *The
Fan* (1714); "your Muse" refers to Gay [3] **plains . . . sport**
The Shepherd's Week (1714) [4] **Phoebus . . . sacred Nine**
Phoebus (Apollo) was the god of poetry; Nine refers to the
nine Muses [5] **guard . . . fair** *i.e.,* the fair one, Caroline, on
her trip to England

Bid the blue *Tritons* sound their twisted shells,
And call'd the *Nereids* from their pearly cells.
   Thus my warm zeal had drawn the Muse along,
Yet knew no method to conduct her song:
I then resolv'd some model to pursue,
Perus'd French criticks, and began anew.
Long open panegyrick drags at best,
And praise is only praise when well address'd.   30
   Straight, *Horace* for some lucky ode I sought:
And all along I trac'd him thought by thought:
This new performance to a friend I show'd;
For shame, says he, what, imitate an ode!
I'd rather ballads write, and *Grubstreet*[6] lays,
Than pillage *Caesar*[7] for my patron's praise:
One common fate all imitators share,
To save mince-pies, and cap the grocer's ware.[8]
Vex'd at the charge, I to the flames commit
Rhymes, similies, Lord's names, and ends of wit;   40
In blotted stanzas scraps of odes expire,
And fustian mounts in pyramids of fire.
   Ladies,[9] to you I next inscrib'd my lay,
And writ a letter in familiar way:
For still impatient till the Princess came,
You from description wish'd to know the dame.
Each day my pleasing labour larger grew,
For still new graces open'd to my view.
Twelve lines ran on to introduce the theme,
And then I thus pursu'd the growing scheme.   50
   Beauty and wit were sure by nature join'd,
And charms are emanations of the mind;
The soul transpiercing through the shining frame,
Forms all the graces of the Princely Dame:
Benevolence her conversation guides,

[6] **Grubstreet** a street in Cripplegate, inhabited by literary hacks. Thus, "Grubstreet," as an adjective, meant the mediocre   [7] **Caesar** Horace praised his patron, Augustus Caesar, in several of his poems. Caesar may also refer to Horace who was supreme among ancient poets   [8] **To save . . . ware** pages of unsold books were used under pies in baking or to wrap groceries   [9] **Ladies** the Maids of Honor at Court

Smiles on her cheek, and in her eye resides.
Such harmony upon her tongue is found,
As softens English *to* Italian *sound:*
Yet in those sounds such sentiments appear,
60 *As charm the judgment, while they sooth the ear.*
    Religion's chearful flame her bosom warms,
Calms all her hours, and brightens all her charms.
Henceforth, ye fair, at chappel mind your pray'rs,
Nor catch your lover's eyes with artful airs;
Restrain your looks, kneel more, and whisper less,
Nor most devoutly criticize on dress.
    From her form all your characters of life,
The tender mother, and the faithful wife.
Oft have I seen her little infant train,
70 *The lovely promise of a future reign;*
Observ'd with pleasure ev'ry dawning grace,
And all the mother op'ning[10] in their face,
The son shall add new honours to the line,
And early with paternal virtues shine;
When he the tale of Audenard [11] *repeats,*
His little heart with emulation beats;
With conquests yet to come his bosom glows,
He dreams of triumphs and of vanquish'd foes.
Each year with arts shall store his rip'ning brain,
80 *And from his grandsire he shall learn to reign.*
    Thus far I'd gone: propitious rising gales
Now bid the sailor hoist the swelling sails.
Fair *Carolina* lands; the cannons roar
White *Albion's*[12] cliffs resound from shore to shore,
Behold the bright original appear,
All praise is faint when *Carolina's* near.
Thus to the nation's joy, but poet's cost,
The Princess came, and my new plan was lost.
    Since all my schemes were baulk'd, my last resort,
90 I left the Muses to frequent the Court;
Pensive each night, from room to room I walk'd,

[10] **op'ning** showing, revealed   [11] **Audenard** Oudenarde, a town
in Belgium, where Marlborough defeated the French in 1708
[12] **Albion** England

To one I bow'd, and with another talk'd;
Enquir'd what news, or such a Lady's name,
And did the next day, and the next, the same.
Places, I found, were daily giv'n away,
And yet no friendly Gazette[13] mention'd *Gay*.
I ask'd a friend what method to pursue;
He cry'd, I want a place as well as you.
Another ask'd me, why I had not writ:
A poet owes his fortune to his wit.   100
Straight I reply'd, with what a courtly grace,
Flows easy verse from him that has a place!
Had *Virgil* ne'er at court improv'd his strains;
He still had sung of flocks and homely swains;
And had not *Horace* sweet preferment found,
The Roman lyre had never learnt to sound.
   Once ladies fair in homely guise I sung,
And with their names wild woods and mountains
   rung.[14]
Oh, teach me now to strike a softer strain!
The Court refines the language of the plain.   110
   You must, cries one, the Ministry rehearse,
And with each patriot's name prolong your verse.
But sure this truth to poets should be known,
That praising all alike, is praising none.
   Another told me, if I wish'd success,
To some distinguish'd Lord I must address;
One whose high virtues speak his noble blood,
One always zealous for his country's good;
Where valour and strong eloquence unite,
In council cautious, resolute in fight;   120
Whose gen'rous temper prompts him to defend,
And patronize the man that wants a friend.
You have, 'tis true, the noble patron shown,
But I, alas! am to *Argyle*[15] unknown.
   Still ev'ry one I met in this agreed,

[13] **Gazette** appointments were announced in the official Court journal, the *London Gazette* [14] **Once . . . rung** Gay's early poems, *The Fan* and *The Shepherd's Week,* were both pastorals [15] **Argyle** the Duke of Argyle was extremely influential at Court in 1714

That writing was my method to succeed;
But now preferments so possess'd my brain,
That scarce I could produce a single strain:
Indeed I sometimes hammer'd out a line,
130 Without connection as without design.
One morn upon the Princess this I writ,
An epigram that boasts more truth than wit.
   The pomp of titles easy faith might shake,
She scorn'd an empire for religion's sake:[16]
For this, on earth, the British *crown is giv'n,*
And an immortal crown decreed in heav'n.
   Again, while George's virtues rais'd my thought,
The following lines prophetick fancy wrought.
   Methinks I see some bard, whose heav'nly rage
140 *Shall rise in song, and warm a future age;*
Look back through time, and, rapt in wonder, trace
The glorious series of the Brunswick *race.*[17]
   From the first George *these godlike kings descend,*
A line which only with the world shall end.
The next a gen'rous Prince renown'd in arms,
And bless'd, long bless'd in Carolina's *charms;*
From these the rest. 'Tis thus secure in peace,
We plow the fields, and reap the year's increase:
Now Commerce, *wealthy goddess, rears her head,*
150 *And bids* Britannia's *fleets their canvas spread;*
Unnumber'd ships the peopled ocean hide,
And wealth returns with each revolving tide.
   Here paus'd the sullen Muse, in haste I dress'd,
And through the croud of needy courtiers press'd;
Though unsuccessful, happy whilst I see,
Those eyes that glad a nation, shine on me.

[16] **She scorn'd . . . sake** in 1704, Caroline refused to become a Catholic at the cost of her impending marriage to the Archduke Charles, later titular King and Emperor of Spain   [17] **Brunswick race** hereditary family name of the Hanoverian Kings

THE HARE AND MANY FRIENDS *

Friendship, like love, is but a name,
Unless to one you stint the flame.
The child, whom many fathers share,
Hath seldom known a father's care;
'Tis thus in friendship; who depend
On many, rarely find a friend.
   A hare, who, in a civil way,
Comply'd with ev'ry thing, like *Gay*,
Was known by all the bestial train,
Who haunt the wood, or graze the plain: 10
Her care was, never to offend,
And ev'ry creature was her friend.
   As forth she went at early dawn
To taste the dew-besprinkled lawn,
Behind she hears the hunter's cries,
And from the deep-mouth'd thunder flies;
She starts, she stops, she pants for breath,
She hears the near advance of death,
She doubles to mis-lead the hound,
And measures back her mazy round;   20
'Till, fainting in the publick way,
Half dead with fear she gasping lay.
   What transport in her bosom grew,
When first the horse appear'd in view!
   Let me, says she, your back ascend,
And owe my safety to a friend,
You know my feet betray my flight,

* From the *Fables*, First Series (1727), dedicated to the Duke of Cumberland, six-year-old son of George II and Caroline. Like *An Epistle to a Lady*, "The Hare and Many Friends" is an overt reminder of Gay's availability for a Court appointment, but in this poem, there is a clear hint, after thirteen years, of the disenchantment which governs much of the social and political satire in *The Beggar's Opera*

To friendship ev'ry burden's light.
   The horse reply'd, poor honest puss,
30   It grieves my heart to see thee thus;
'   Be comforted, relief is near;
For all your friends are in the rear.
   She next the stately bull implor'd;
And thus reply'd the, mighty lord.
Since ev'ry beast alive can tell
That I sincerely wish you well,
I may, without offence, pretend
To take the freedom of a friend;
Love calls me hence; a fav'rite cow
40   Expects me near yon barley mow:
And when a lady's in the case,
You know, all other things give place.
To leave you thus might seem unkind
But see, the goat is just behind.
   The goat remark'd her pulse was high,[2]
Her languid head, her heavy eye;
My back, says she, may do you harm;
The sheep's at hand, and wool is warm.
   The sheep was feeble, and complain'd,
50   His sides a load of wool sustain'd,
Said he was slow, confest his fears;
For hounds eat sheep as well as hares.
   She now the trotting calf addrest,
To save from death a friend distrest.
   Shall I, says he, of tender age,
In this important care engage?
Older and abler past you by;
How strong are those! how weak am I!
Should I presume to bear you hence,
60   Those friends of mine may take offence.
Excuse me then. You know my heart.
But dearest friends, alas, must part!
How shall we all lament: adieu.
For see the hounds are just in view.

[2] **The goat . . . high** *i.e.* the goat noticed that the hare's pulse,
etc.

From GAY'S LETTERS [*]

To Swift, June 8, 1714. I am every day attending my
Lord Treasurer for his bounty in order to set me out,[1]
which he hath promised me upon the following peti-
tion which I sent him by Dr. Arbuthnot.[2]

The Epigrammatical Petition of John Gay.

I'm no more to converse with the swains[3]
But go where fine people resort
One can live without money on plains
But never without it at Court.

If when with the swains I did gambol
I arrayd me in silver and blue[4]
When abroad and in Courts I shall ramble
Pray, my Lord, how much money will do?

To Swift, December 22, 1722. I lodge at present in
Burlington House[5] and have received many civilitys
from many great men but very few real benefits. They
wonder at each other for not providing for me and I
wonder at 'em all. Experience has given me some
knowledge of them, so that I can say that 'tis not in
their power to disappoint me.

---

[*] Gay had been appointed secretary to the mission headed by
Lord Clarendon which went to Hanover in the summer of 1714
in an effort to sway the Elector, George Lewis, later George I,
to the Tory party. Gay had been promised 100 pounds for
traveling expenses which the Lord Treasurer, Robert Harley,
Earl of Oxford, Gay's friend and fellow-Scriblerian ultimately
paid him   [2] Dr. John Arbuthnot, physician, man of letters, and
friend to Gay, Pope, Swift; the addressee of Pope's famous
Epistle   [3] Gay's pastoral poem, *The Shepherd's Week*   [4] See
the Prologue to *The Shepherd's Week*, line 40   [5] See p. 80, n.
33

To Swift, February 3, 1723. As for the reigning amusement of the town, 'tis entirely musick, real fiddles, bass viols and hautboys[6] not poetical harps, lyres, and reeds. There's nobody allow'd to say I sing but an eunuch or an Italian woman. Every body is grown now as great a judge of musick as they were in your time of poetry and folks that could not distinguish one tune from another now daily dispute about the different styles of Hendel, Bononcini, and Attillio.[7] People have now forgot Homer and Virgil and Caesar, or at least they have lost their ranks for in London and Westminster in all polite conversations, Senesino[8] is daily voted to be the greatest man that ever liv'd. I am oblig'd to you for your advice, as I have been formerly for your assistance in introducing me into business. I shall this year be a Commissioner of the State Lottery[9] which will be worth to me a hundred and fifty pounds and I am not without hopes that I have friends that will think of some better and more certain provision for me.

To Mrs. Howard,[10] August, 1723. I have long wish'd to be able to put in practice that valuable worldly qualification of being insincere. One of my chief reasons is that I hate to be particular and I think if a man cannot conform to the customs of the world, he is not fit to be encourag'd or to live in it. I know that if one would be agreeable to men of dignity one must study to imitate them, and I know which way they get money and places. I cannot indeed wonder that the talents requisite for a great statesman are so scarce in the world since so many of those who possess them

[6] hautboys oboes   [7] **Bononcini, Attilio** like Handel, composers of Italian Opera   [8] **Senesino** a leading singer in Italian Opera   [9] A post which Gay held from 1723-1731, his only Court appointment   [10] Henrietta Howard, Maid of Honor to the Princess Caroline and mistress to the Prince of Wales (later George II), was Gay's friend at Court. There is something ludicrous about Gay's lecturing Mrs. Howard, who had grown wise in the ways of a Court, on how to get along in the world

are every month cut off in the prime of their age at the
Old-Bailey. How envious are statesmen and how jealous are they of rivals! A highway-man never picks up
an honest man for a companion, but if such a one ac-
cidentally falls in his way, if he cannot turn his heart,
he, like a wise statesman, discards him.

To William Fortescue, September 23, 1725. I am
again returned to Twickenham,[11] upon the news of
the person's death you wrote to me about.[12] I cannot
say I have any great prospect of success, but the affair remains yet undetermined and I cannot tell who
will be his successor. I know I have sincerely your
good wishes upon all occasions. One would think that
my friends use[13] me to disappointments to try how
many I could bear. If they do so, they are mistaken,
for as I don't expect much, I can never be much disappointed.

To Swift (joint letter with Pope), October 22, 1727.
The Queen's family[14] is at last settled and in the list,
I was appointed Gentleman-Usher to the Princess
Louisa, the youngest Princess, which, upon account
that I am so far advanc'd in life,[15] I have declin'd ac-
cepting and have endeavour'd, in the best manner I
could, to make my excuses to her Majesty. So now all
my expectations are vanish'd and I have no prospect
but in depending wholly upon my self and my own
conduct. As I am us'd to disappointments, I can bear
them, but as I can have no more hopes, I can no more
be disappointed, so that I am in a blessed condition.
You remember you were advising me to go into Newgate to finish my scenes the more correctly[16]—I now

[11] **Twickenham** Pope's villa near London   [12] Gay had returned
in haste to London from Wiltshire on receipt of Fortescue's
news that an appointment might be available   [13] **use** to expose
regularly   [14] **Queen's family** the new Queen's Court appointments   [15] Gay was then forty-two   [16] Swift was in England during the summer while Gay was working on *The Beggar's Opera*

think I shall, for I have no attendance to hinder me, but my Opera is already finished.

To Edward Harley, Earl of Oxford,[17] *February 12, 1728.* I was last night to pay my duty to your Lordship and to thank you for interesting yourself in so kind a manner in my behalf. I had heard before that the King and Queen were to be present at Julius Caesar on Friday, so that my intention was to acquaint your Lordship that I had fixt on Thursday. As to the boxes on that day,[18] I fear by what I have heard about the town, they are taken up already, but if your Lordship would be so good as to send a servant to the box-keeper, I hope I shall have the honour of Lady Oxford's presence in the very box she chooses, for I know Mr. Rich would upon all occasions be very glad to oblige your Lordship.

To Swift, February 15, 1728. I have deferr'd writing to you from time to time till I could give you an account of the Beggar's Opera. It is acted at the playhouse in Lincoln's Inn Fields with such success that the playhouse hath been crouded every night. To night is the fifteenth time of acting and 'tis thought it will run a fortnight longer. I have order'd Motte[19] to send the play to you the first opportunity. I made no interest either for approbation or money nor hath any body been prest to take tickets for my Benefit,[20] notwithstanding which, I think I shall make an addition to my fortune of between six and seven hundred pounds. I know this account will give you pleasure, as

[17] Son of the Lord Treasurer, Gay's early friend [18] **boxes . . . that day** box seats at the Theatre Royal for *The Beggar's Opera*. As is the case with a "smash" hit, tickets for *The Beggar's Opera* were hard to come by. The play's appeal was such that even royalty could not resist—the King and Queen attended a performance on February 22, 1728 [19] Swift's publisher [20] **Benefit** during the run of a successful play, special performances were held, on designated nights, for the author's benefit

I have push'd through this precarious affair without servility or flattery. As to any favours from great men, I am in the same state you left me, but I am a great deal happier as I have no expectations. . . . Lord Cobham says that I should have printed it [*The Beggar's Opera*] in Italian over against the English, that the ladys might have understood what they read. The outlandish (as they now call it) Opera hath been so thin[21] of late that some have call'd that the Beggar's Opera and if the run continues, I fear I shall have remonstrances drawn up against me by the Royal Academy of Musick.[22]

To Swift, March 20, 1728. The Beggar's Opera hath now been acted thirty six times and was as full the last night as the first and as yet, there is not the least probability of a thin audience, though there is a discourse about the town that the Directors of the Royal Academy of Musick design to solicit against its being play'd on the outlandish Opera days, as it is now call'd. On the Benefit day of one of the actresses last week, one of the players falling sick, they were oblig'd to give out[23] another play or dismiss the audience. A play was given out but the people call'd out for the Beggar's Opera and they were forc'd to play it or the audience would not have stay'd. I have got, by all this success, between seven and eight hundred pounds and Rich (deducting the whole charges of the house) hath clear'd already near four thousand pounds. . . . There is a mezzo-tinto[24] print publish'd to day of Polly, the heroine of the Beggar's Opera, who was before unknown and is now in so high vogue, that I am in doubt whether her fame does not surpass that of the Opera itself.[25]

[21] **thin** poorly attended   [22] The Royal Academy sponsored the Italian Opera   [23] **give out** schedule or announce   [24] **mezzotint** engraving   [25] Lavinia Fenton, the actress who played Polly Peachum, was the rage of London during the winter and spring of 1728. In the role of Polly, her charms caught the eye of the Duke of Bolton who ultimately made her his Duchess

To Swift, May 16, 1728. The Beggar's Opera is acted here[26] but our Polly here hath got no fame, but the actors have got money. I have sent by Dr. Delany, the Opera, Polly Peachum, and Captain Macheath.[27] I would have sent you my own head[28] which is now graving to make up the gang, but it is not yet finish'd. I suppose you must have heard that I have had the honour to have had a sermon preach'd against my works by a Court chaplain, which I look upon as no small addition to my fame.[29]

To Swift, December 2, 1728. I have been confin'd about ten days but never to my bed, so that I hope soon to get abroad about my business, which is, the care of the second part of the Beggar's Opera[30] which was almost ready for rehearsal. But Rich receiv'd the Duke of Grafton's[31] commands (upon an information he was rehearsing a play improper to be represented) not to rehearse any new play whatever 'till his Grace hath seen it. What will become of it, I know not but I am sure I have written nothing that can be legally supprest, unless the setting vices in general in an odious light and virtue in an amiable one may give offence.

To Swift, March 18, 1729. You must undoubtedly have heard that the Duchess[32] took up my defense with the King and Queen in the cause of my play and that she hath been forbid the Court for interesting

[26] Gay was writing from Bath, the famous eighteenth-century resort [27] Opera . . . Macheath a copy of the play and engravings of Polly and Macheath [28] my own head an engraving of himself [29] In March, Dr. Thomas Herring, the King's Chaplain, delivered a sermon in Lincoln's Inn Chapel condemning *The Beggar's Opera* for presenting crime in a favorable light. Swift wrote a defense of Gay for the *Dublin Intelligencer,* May 25, 1728, "A Vindication of Mr. Gay and *The Beggar's Opera*" [30] *Polly,* written as a sequel to *The Beggar's Opera* [31] The Lord Chamberlain who served as the Royal censor. Ten days later, the Duke, no doubt on Walpole's prompting, banned the production of *Polly* [32] The Duchess of Queensberry

herself to increase my fortune for the publication of it without being acted. The Duke too hath given up his employment[33] which he would have done if the Duchess had not met this treatment, upon account of ill usage from the Ministers but this hasten'd him in what he had determin'd. The play is now almost printed with the musick, words, and basses engrav'd on 31 copper plates which, by my friend's assistance, hath a probability to turn greatly to my advantage.[34] . . . For writing in the cause of virtue and against the fashionable vices, I am look'd upon at present as the most obnoxious person almost in England.

To Swift, November 9, 1729. Next week I believe I shall be in town, not at Whitehall for those lodgings were judg'd not convenient for me and dispos'd of.[35] . . . You have often twitted me in the teeth with hankering after the Court. In that you mistook me, for I know by experience that there is no dependence that can be sure but a dependence upon ones-self.

[33] employment his Royal appointments [34] In its printed form, *Polly* brought Gay some 1200 pounds, more than he could have hoped for had the play been produced [35] Because of *Polly*, Gay was dispossessed of the apartment at Whitehall to which he was entitled as Commissioner of the Lottery

BIBLIOGRAPHY

ABOUT GAY

Dobson, Austin, "John Gay" in *Dictionary of National Biography* (London, 1921-22), Vol. VII.

Herbert, A. P., *Mr. Gay's London* (London, 1948).

Irving, William H., *John Gay, Favorite of the Wits* (Duke, 1940).

Johnson, Samuel, "John Gay" in *Lives of the English Poets*, ed. George Birkbeck Hill (Oxford, 1905).

Melville, Lewis, *Life and Letters of John Gay* (London, 1921).

The Letters of John Gay, ed. C. F. Burgess (Clarendon Press, 1966).

ABOUT *THE BEGGAR'S OPERA*

Bronson, Bertrand H., "The Beggar's Opera" in *University of California Publications in English* (California, 1941), Vol. VIII.

Burgess, C. F., "Political Satire: John Gay's *The Beggar's Opera*," *The Midwest Quarterly*, VI (1965), 265-276.

Empson, William, "The Beggar's Opera" in *Some Versions of Pastoral* (London, 1935).

Handley-Taylor, Geoffrey and Barber, F. G., *John Gay and the Ballad Opera* (London, 1956).

Kidson, Frank, *The Beggar's Opera, Its Predecessors and Successors* (Cambridge, Eng., 1922).

Schultz, William E., *Gay's Beggar's Opera, Its Content, History and Influence* (Yale, 1923).

GENERAL CRITICISM

Armens, Sven M., *John Gay, Social Critic* (Columbia, 1954).

Bateson, F. W., *English Comic Drama, 1700-1750* (Oxford, 1929).

Brown, Wallace C., "Gay's Mastery of the Heroic Couplet," *PMLA,* LXI (1946), 114-125.

Irving, William H., *John Gay's London* (Harvard, 1928).

Spacks, Patricia Meyer, "John Gay: A Satirist's Progress," *Essays in Criticism,* XIV (1964), 156-170.

Sutherland, James R., "John Gay" in *Eighteenth-Century English Literature,* ed. James L. Clifford (New York, 1959).